JOYFULLY FOLLOWING

JOYFULLY FOLLOWING

Aletha Hinthorn

Beacon Hill Press of Kansas City
Kansas City, Missouri

Copyright 1996
by Aletha Hinthorn

ISBN 083-411-6065

Printed in the
United States of America

Cover design: Paul Franitza
Cover Photo: Index Stock

Library of Congress Cataloging-in-Publication Data
Hinthorn, Aletha.
    Joyfully following / Aletha Hinthorn.
        p.   cm. — (Satisfied heart series)
    Includes bibliographical references.
    ISBN 0-8341-1606-5 (pbk.)
    1. Christian life—Study and teaching.   2. Obedience—Religious aspects—Christianity—Study and teaching.   3. God—Will—Study and teaching.   4. Trust in God—Study and teaching. I. Title. II. Series: Hinthorn, Aletha. Satisfied heart series.
BV4501.2.H5225   1996
248.4—dc20   96-12706
                                                                              CIP

10   9   8   7   6   5   4

Contents

1

FOLLOWING CHRIST— THE REAL JOY

God is the absolutely real one; when he enters a person's life, it is we who are suddenly aware of our tentative and fragile existence.[1]

—*William Dyrness*

Introduction

When I was a girl on the farm, I loved to take a shopping trip to St. Louis. Several times a year my mother and I traveled 60 miles to the big city to spend a day browsing the sale racks. On one occasion as we returned home with packages heaped on the backseat, excitement waning, I felt a strange emptiness. Shopping had been exciting, and opening the packages would be fun, but I sensed that there must be more to life than just experiences and a collection of objects in order to satisfy.

God has "set eternity in the hearts of men" (Eccles. 3:11). We were created with a longing for the spiritual world, so we can never be satisfied with the material world alone. If the Holy Spirit is not a reality in our lives, we will seek spiritual realities elsewhere.

Solomon declared, "I denied myself nothing my eyes desired; I refused my heart no pleasure. . . . Yet when I surveyed all that my hands had done and what I had toiled to

achieve, everything was meaningless" (Eccles. 2:10-11).
Solomon experienced everything possible to do and found
it all to be without meaning.

Discussion and Questions

How can we discern what truly satisfies? What gives real joy and what is meaningless in the end? God wants to
teach us to recognize Satan's whispers of "Here—eat this,
and you will live."

To the Old Testament writers, a person was truly living
when God the Father approved everything he or she did. "In
his favour is life" (Ps. 30:5, KJV), wrote the psalmist. Life,
then, to the biblical writers, stood for spiritual life—vitality,
joy, satisfaction, and a sense of well-being.

Let's first explore the biblical definition of true life and
discover how we can enter this life. We'll also examine how
we can experience true life.

◆ Exploring True Life

1. God warned Adam and Eve not to eat of the tree of
the knowledge of good and evil, because they would die
upon doing so. See Gen. 2:17. In what way do you think
they died that day?

2. It is interesting to notice what Jesus called physical
death. See Luke 8:52-55 and John 11:11-13. Do you think
He was implying that real death is spiritual death, rather
than physical?

3. In Gen. 3:4-5, Satan insinuated that their lives would be greatly improved with the knowledge of good and evil. What three things made Satan's offer tempting to Eve? See verse 6.

4. Satan still tempts people to look for satisfaction in the wrong places. According to the following verses, what do people think will bring them a satisfying life?

 Eccles. 2:1-11

 Luke 12:15

 1 Tim. 5:6

5. "My people . . . have forsaken me, the spring of living water, and have dug their own cisterns, broken cisterns that cannot hold water" (Jer. 2:13). What are some of the "broken cisterns" that people today expect to quench their thirst?

A recent periodical stated, "Most people seek happiness outside themselves—more money, a better job, more sex—but there's no true contentment unless it first comes from within." The authors stated that today's stresses require a "strong, solid sense of self."[2] At first we might think these authors are correct, but Jesus said, "You have no life in you" (John 6:53). In ourselves we find no life. It's only as He is living in us that we have life.

6. What we long to experience is not our own life, but Christ's. "I no longer live, but Christ lives in me," wrote Paul in Gal. 2:20. As we live out God's Word, the unbelievable happens. We actually share in His divine nature. We're not just improving our life—we're letting Christ live in us. See 2 Pet. 1:3-4.

7. What terms did Jesus use to promise that the life He gives will be satisfying? See John 4:14 and 6:35.

8. Jesus came to give us life. "The thief comes only to steal and kill and destroy; I have come that they may have life, and have it to the full" (John 10:10). Describe the qualities of life that Jesus came to give.

 John 14:27

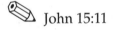 John 15:11

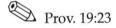 Prov. 19:23

9. Physical life exists on this earth, where things are seen, but God calls us to a new Kingdom, where the invisible is more real than the visible. What contrast is made in 2 Cor. 4:18?

God does not want us to be deceived so that at the end of our lives we say, "I thought what I was doing was real and had value, but all was 'meaningless, a chasing after the wind.'" See Eccles. 1:14. Our spirits hunger for something that is authentic—not an illusion or a counterfeit, but the deeply satisfying answer to an inner craving.

◆ Living Out This True Life

One spring about 15 years ago, God began teaching me the process of finding life—abundant life. Solomon's words at the end of Ecclesiastes captivated my attention: "Fear God and keep his commandments, for this is the whole duty of man" (12:13).

For months the Holy Spirit kept these words close to my heart and whispered again and again, "You have no duty other than My commands. I'm not giving you one thing to do other than what I've already commanded you in Scripture. Before you do something, find out if it's one of My commands. If it's not, it simply isn't your duty."

I discovered a heart hunger to find a scriptural reason for everything I did. If God didn't say to do it, it wasn't my assignment, and I knew it would bring no fulfillment or satisfaction.

It wasn't hard to find scriptural reasons to clean house, to care for and to love my children and husband. Other daily activities, such as shopping and being with others, went through this scrutiny. Relationships and activities became opportunities to apply Scripture.

Jesus had said that if I abided in Him and His Word abided in me, He would give me His joy (John 15:10-11). Sometimes I thought I'd burst with His joy. I could agree fully with Jeremiah: "Your words . . . were my joy and my heart's delight" (15:16).

1. Notice how other biblical writers revered God's Word.

Job 23:12

 Ps. 119:72

 2 Sam. 22:31; Ps. 12:6

God says our only duty is to fear Him and keep His commandments. If the incentive for all we do is not obedience to the Word, eventually we'll agree with Solomon: it is all hollow and worthless.

Jesus promises, "For my flesh is real food and my blood is real drink" (John 6:55). He is saying, "Partake of Me, and you will be truly satisfied."

2. Jesus' promise of "real food" and "real drink" stands in contrast to Solomon's frequent use of "meaningless." (For instance, see Eccles. 1:14 and 12:8.)

"Unless you eat the flesh of the Son of Man and drink his blood, you have no life in you" (John 6:53). We must take in His flesh and blood to know the reality of living in Christ. According to the *Jewish New Testament Commentary*, "To eat the flesh of the Son of Man is to absorb his entire way of being and living."[3]

3. What do you think might be involved in absorbing Jesus' way of living?

4. Our spirits survive only on truth. It's interesting that all countries have a form of bread. Just as our bodies must have bread, so our spirits depend on *spiritual bread* (truth) for survival. See Matt. 4:4. Discuss what you think it means to let the Word become flesh within us.

The *Jewish New Testament Commentary* also states that to drink His blood is to absorb His self-sacrificing life-motivation.[4] In fact, to drink His blood means to absorb His very life, since "the life of the flesh is in the blood" (Lev. 17:11, KJV). To drink His blood, then, means we're willing to be motivated by the same self-sacrificing spirit Jesus had.

Another way to restate Lev. 17:11 is to say that the joy (life) of our obeying the Law (flesh) is in our motivation (blood). We don't find joy in living out Christ's commands if we obey them with a rebellious spirit. If someone demands obedience, and we obey against our wills, we find no deep satisfaction in conforming.

Real joy comes as we are motivated by love and as we willingly obey the One who sacrificed His life for us. We surrender our own desires because we love Him.

5. Restate what you understand it means to drink Jesus' blood.

6. What, according to Jesus, was the food that satisfied Him? See John 4:34. What does this say about what will give life to us?

In the Old Testament, God satisfied the Israelites' hunger with manna. See Exod. 16:4. After that, the Jews had a tradition that said, "As the first Redeemer caused the manna to fall from heaven, even so the second Redeemer will cause the manna to fall."[5] Manna became a favorite topic among the Jewish commentators.

Philo, a Jewish philosopher who lived before Christ, explained, "When the people sought what it was that feeds the soul they found it is the utterance of God. . . . This is the heavenly food."[6] Manna that the second Redeemer (Jesus) would provide would be the utterance of God.

7. In John 6:54 the verb "eat" not only expresses the simple act of consuming but also includes the process of savoring or dwelling upon with pleasure. This verb also means the process is continuous—it is not done once for all time. What do these concepts teach about our intake of the Word?

8. We can approach our "heavenly food" with the same eagerness we have when we sit down to a Thanksgiving dinner. What foods are the scriptures compared to in the following verses?

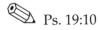 Ps. 19:10

 Isa. 55:1-2

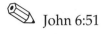 John 6:51

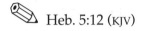 Heb. 5:12 (KJV)

Give thanks for every desire you have to feed on God's Word—our "real food" and "real drink." Ask Him to increase your anticipation to hear Him speak through the Word. "Pay attention to what I say; listen closely to my words . . . for they are life to those who find them" (Prov. 4:20, 22).

If you awaken in the mornings feeling down in your spirit, glance at Scripture verses while getting dressed. You can find joy by feeding on His Word.

9. We must assimilate God's Word into our lives in order to experience His life. It's possible to look at food, study it, and even serve it to others without taking it into our own bodies and receiving nourishment from it. Using this comparison, what's the key to making His Word become life within us? See John 5:38.

10. The Word doesn't become life within us until it takes root within us. See Matt. 13:21. What do you think it means for the Word to take root in us?

11. To eat Jesus' flesh means that we absorb His way of thinking and living. In other words, we obey His Word. To drink Jesus' blood means that we obey His Word out of a self-sacrificing motivation.

We can use these two concepts hundreds of times a day as we make choices for life. List several things you will do today. What scriptural reasons can you find to do them?

Offer those activities as your gift to the Lord. "And whatever you do, whether in word or deed, do it all in the name of the Lord Jesus" (Col. 3:17). The joy of obedience may surprise you!

Scriptural Role Model

John wrote that the Word of God became flesh and dwelt among us. Then Paul wrote what must have been startling words to the Jews: "Christ lives in me" (Gal. 2:20).

Christ lives in us as we learn to live out His Word. This is not some mystical kind of union, but a deep consciousness that we are living out the will of God. To the extent that we obey Scripture, we are His Word become flesh.

How blessed Mary was to have produced a holy son in cooperation with the Spirit! Christ lived in her physical body, but Christ will also be the life of our spiritual bodies.

Jesus' physical life was formed in Mary because of her faith and obedience. "Blessed is she who has believed that what the Lord has said to her will be accomplished!" (Luke 1:45). When we can say with Paul, "Christ lives in me," it's because the Word lives in us through our faith and obedience.

Through the ages Mary has been called blessed, because the Word became flesh within her. But even now, we who let the Word dwell in us are also blessed.

Memorize

"Take to heart all the words I have solemnly declared to you. . . . They are not just idle words for you—they are your life" (Deut. 32:46-47).

Prayer

Dear Lord, in myself I find no life. I want to abide in You and to find my highest satisfaction in doing the Father's will, just as You do. Letting Your Word become flesh within me is all that truly satisfies. Thank You for teaching me to find real joy in You. I praise You in Jesus' name. Amen.

2

BE ASSURED—
HE IS GUIDING YOU

If a man does not believe that all the world is as God's family, where nothing happens by chance, but all is guided and directed by the care and providence of a being that is all love and goodness to all his creatures; if a man does not believe this from his heart, he cannot be said to believe in God.[1]

—*William Law*

Introduction

"Play something for me," directed Professor Spector at my first piano lesson at Pittsburg State University in Kansas. I launched into parts of Beethoven's *Sonata Pathetique*. I say "parts," because my previous piano teacher had wanted two students to play the sonata at our recital, so she had divided it between us.

About midway through, Professor Spector abruptly stopped me. "Why are you playing only parts of this sonata?" he demanded. I explained about the recital and the need to cut parts here and there.

The professor began pacing the floor, irate because of the musical atrocity I had committed. "Do you realize that chopping a Beethoven sonata is like whacking away on a fine painting?" he said, pointing to a picture on his wall.

He was right. A master painter has a purpose for every brush stroke, just as a good composer or author never inserts irrelevant details. That's what we expect from human creators, yet we sometimes accuse our loving Creator of allowing irrelevant, insignificant sections in our lives. However, Eph. 2:10 says that we are God's *poema*—the Greek word for poem, a literary form in which every word is placed with exacting precision. "We are God's *[poema]* . . . to do good works, which God prepared in advance for us to do."

Since each of us is God's poem, we can have faith that He has carefully selected each detail of our lives. Only when looking back over our lives will we be able to detect the significance of some of the details. The significance of other details will remain a mystery to us until we get to heaven. But by faith we can gratefully accept all as coming from a loving Father's hand.

Discussion and Questions

What satisfaction we find in knowing our steps are ordered by a loving Creator—a Creator whose promises to direct us flow from His love! What else could His motivation be? Which of us cares about the trivial concerns of strangers? The more we love someone, though, the more we care about that person's interests and want to help him or her make right choices.

In this chapter we'll see that God's love is over all, that Satan's power is limited, and that God's presence is in every circumstance.

◆ God's Love Over All

1. God controls every detail of our lives because He loves us so much. He continually expresses His love in new ways. In fact, He has promised never to stop doing good to us. He constantly surrounds us with His favor as a shield, so that all that comes to us must come through His shield of love. See Jer. 32:40-41 and Ps. 5:12 for these promises of His unceasing and all-encompassing protection.

2. What do you find in the following verses about God's tender care being over every detail of our lives?

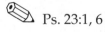 Ps. 23:1, 6

 Ps. 34:9-10

 Matt. 10:29-31

 2 Cor. 9:8

3. When God moves, He controls every detail. Nothing stands in His way. What details recorded in Exod. 12:36, 41-42 indicated that God was in control?

4. God "is the blessed controller of all things" (1 Tim. 6:15, PHILLIPS). Read this verse in other versions. List three areas of your life that you are thankful God controls.

5. How does recognizing that He is the Blessed Controller encourage you?

6. To demonstrate how carefully God protects us, He says He guards us as He guards the apple of His eye. (The apple is the pupil, or the center, of the eye.) See Deut. 32:10 and Zech. 2:8.

7. Our natural instinct is to protect our eyes above all other members of our bodies. Also, our pupils are helpless to protect themselves. What does this say about God's protection of us?

"He leads me . . . for his name's sake" (Ps. 23:3, NKJV)—not for mine, but all for His name's sake. He loves us so much that to lead us is His doing something for himself.

8. According to Ps. 35:27, what does God delight in? What does that tell us about God's desire to lovingly guard and guide every detail of our lives?

9. Review two of God's promises to lead us. Memorize at least one of them.

 Ps. 32:8

 Isa. 48:17

◆ God's Limits on Satan's Power

1. Even though Satan often exercises power, God is still in control. He has set definite boundaries on Satan's power. What did Paul say hindered him from seeing the Thessalonians? See 1 Thess. 2:18.

R. C. H. Lenski comments on this verse: "Satan succeeded in frustrating Paul's two plans to return to Thessalonica, but only because this accorded with God's own plan regarding the work Paul was to do. Satan has brought many a martyr to his death, and God permitted it. The death of these martyrs was more blessed for them and for the cause of the gospel than their lives would have been. It is ever so with Satan's successes. No thanks to Satan! His guilt is the greater."[2]

2. Satan may appear to have the upper hand for a time, but to those who trust God to work in every detail, he only *appears* to be in control. What was Paul's bold assertion in 2 Cor. 2:14?

3. Let's consider some of the times God used Satan's worst deeds for His purposes. Read the following verses and identify what Satan did and the glory that God gained through it.

 1 Chron. 21:1, 22-25; 2 Chron. 3:1

(Scholars say that David's fear of the angel of destruction caused him to offer sacrifice there and to continue to do so later. Eventually this site was chosen for the Temple.)

 Job 1:6-12; 42:10-17

John 13:27 (Although Satan meant this for evil, what good has come to us from it?)

4. The moment we trust God in our situation, Satan's plans are thwarted. God begins to glorify himself in our circumstances. Our problem is that often we don't turn to God and trust Him to take control as David did in 1 Chron. 21:8. Or we don't say, as Job did, "Though He slay me, yet will I trust Him" (Job 13:15, NKJV).

Read Phil. 1:12-19. Notice that at the time Paul wrote Philippians, he was in prison; however, he said, "My chains are in Christ (Christ's will for me), so I'm rejoicing, because now Christ is being preached." What were some of the good results Paul could see from his imprisonment?

5. Do you have difficulty seeing God as the Blessed Controller in bad situations? In the following passages, God was praised for being the One who provided all— both good and bad.

 Gen. 45:5-8 (Joseph)

Job 1:21; 2:10; 42:11 (Job)

 John 18:11 (Jesus)

6. What difference do you think it made in these three, because they saw God in control of all that came to them?

7. Before Satan could touch Job he had to ask God's permission and stay within the boundaries God set. Satan still seeks to harm God's children. Although our troubles may originate with Satan or the sin of other people, God allows only those troubles that bring glory to himself when we continue to trust through trial.

According to Isa. 43:2, what protection does He promise us?

8. To the Hebrews, fire and water represented the most severe trials they could pass through in life. God promised the Hebrews that even though they might pass through miserable experiences, no lasting harm would come to them. How does trusting God to be in control affect our ability to live a life that pleases Him?

◆ God's Presence in Every Circumstance

1. Seeing God in everything is the only way to find a completely restful life. According to Exod. 13:21-22, what did God give the Israelites to guide them? What did this say to them about God's guidance?

 He'll shield you from the scorching sun and gives fire for the cold dark night

2. Jesus was perfectly attuned to God's guidance. What phrase does He say twice in John 7:6, 8?

 Go

3. In John 7:6, in what way did Jesus say He differed from the disciples? What do you think He meant?

Perhaps Jesus was saying that all of His decisions about timing mattered. He was trusting God for every choice He made, every word He spoke, every detail of His life. The disciples weren't constantly looking to God to direct their way.

4. What does Prov. 3:5-6 say we must do for God to lead? What does it mean to *acknowledge* someone?

know he is present and just look up and say you are here

God does what we trust Him to do. Do you believe a loving God controls every detail of your life? If you believe He is doing that for you, then He is!

God delights in giving moment-by-moment guidance to those who look to Him. Trust and praise Him for the guidance He'll give today—the interruptions, the help in your work, the interactions with others.

Those who seek God with all their hearts find Him. And if our seeking Him includes looking for Him in the ordinary routine of our everyday lives, we will find Him there.

According to Evelyn Christenson, prisoners who accept Christ while incarcerated often pray, "God, get me out of this hellhole." If God doesn't, their response to His refusal is, "If that's the kind of God I'm serving now, I don't want anything to do with Him anymore. He let me down."

Frequently, however, inmates who have recently become Christians share that they have already grasped that God knows what He is doing, it is for their ultimate good, and they can trust Him completely. Then their response to God is, "Thanks, God, for leaving me here. You have a purpose. What is it?"[3]

5. A key truth God teaches us through His Word is that when we're living in the Spirit, all our circumstances help us. God can make all things, even others' sins, "work together for good to those who love God, . . . who are the called according to His purpose" (Rom. 8:28, NKJV). What does the next verse (v. 29) say is God's purpose?

God's purpose is not to make us successful, rich, or even happy. His purpose is to make us more like Jesus. In all our troubles, God's great objective is to make us mature in Christ. He knows that as we exercise faith and depend upon His power and deliverance, we gain spiritual strength.

6. Since God plans for all our circumstances to help us be more like His Son, we are to be grateful for all of them. God wants us to live with a continual attitude of thanksgiving. See Heb. 13:15 and 1 Thess. 5:18.

7. God leads us not merely to accept what comes but also to praise Him as we begin to see that His mercies really are over all His works. We can be truly thankful for all things, knowing that God allows only what He can use to bring glory to himself and good to us. What Satan intends for evil, God has plans to use for our good. See Jer 29:11.

8. Before we can give thanks for all things, we must believe several concepts about God: He is sovereign (has ultimate control), loving, and faithful. In what ways are you most likely to doubt God when bad things happen in your life?

9. Why is it easier to give thanks when we have faith that God is all-powerful and loving?

When we get to heaven and review our lives from God's perspective, we'll find that His watchful, overruling presence was working in the very places in which we least suspected it.

Scriptural Role Model

Job was a good, righteous, and holy man who lost everything. If one-tenth of Job's troubles happened to one of us, what would be our response? Would we do what Job did upon hearing of his losses? Before he said a thing, "he fell to the ground in worship" (Job 1:20). Job saw God as the Blessed Controller of all things, so he worshiped.

Even though Job made a godly response, his problems didn't go away. His three "friendly enemies" accused him of having hidden sin, or of having parents who had sinned.

In a most wrenching passage, Job wished he had never been born. In effect, God said to him, "You're holding on to one more thing—your need to know the 'why' of your circumstances. Your job is to trust Me."

Finally Job said, "Yes, God, You alone are in control." Then God handed back to Job all he had lost and more—another lesson to Job that God really was in control.

God carefully weighs every burden He puts on us and will never put on us more than we can bear nor more than He can make work for our ultimate good and His glory.

"Thanks be to God, who gives us the victory" (1 Cor. 15:57, NASB).

Memorize

"The LORD will guide you always; he will satisfy your needs in a sun-scorched land and will strengthen your frame" (Isa. 58:11).

Prayer

Dear loving Father, I praise You because Your mercies cover all Your works. You are always doing good to me, and, by faith I say, Thank You, Lord, for all You are allowing in my life at this moment. Give me grace to not look at my failures and problems but to only see Your mercy and Your tender love that richly provide all I need. In Jesus' kind name I pray. Amen.

3 *Oct 20th*

HIS WILL—MY HIGHEST JOY

We "delight" to do the will of God, not because our piety is so exalted, but because we have the sense to see that His will is the best; and therefore what He wants we want also.[1]

—Hannah Whitall Smith

Introduction

"Every Sunday for years my husband's parents have had a big dinner at one o'clock in the afternoon, and Jon wants to go," Joanne shared over the phone. "He doesn't ask me— he just says, 'Let's go.' I think he should want to spend the time building our relationship. It's not that we go every week, but it's always looming up. I don't know what to do about it. It's really a bone of contention in our marriage." Then she laughed and said, "Sundays come up so often."

"Is pleasing God your deepest desire in this situation?" I asked her. "If you can focus on whether or not God is pleased with your attitude, then you are making a clear channel through which God can work. God can give you so much grace for those Sunday dinners that you'll begin to look forward to them, because the joy of the Lord will accompany your obedience."

Several weeks later Joanne said, "I'm really trying to submit about those Sunday dinners and to tell the Lord, 'It doesn't matter if we go or not. I care only that You approve of my attitude.' It's working out much better, but what's really great is that I'm able to say, 'My concern is that God be pleased. That's all I care about.'"

"Finding your joy in pleasing Him by offering up this thing that is most difficult for you is the highest way you can tell God you love Him," I told her. When we offer up our desires simply out of love for Him, He accepts our offerings as gifts of love.

Discussion and Questions

Several years ago my husband suggested we each share something for which we were thankful. I've thought often of my mother's statement. After mentioning several things for which she was grateful, she added, "If I know that God is pleased with me, then let other things fall where they will—I am happy."

Too often, though, our interpretation of submission to God does not include the joy of obedience. "OK—I'll submit," we glumly acknowledge, but we find no joy, no delighting in the law of the Lord.

In this chapter we'll discuss steps necessary to discovering the life of joy—a complete surrender to God's will and a daily choice to have the mind of Christ.

◆ Surrender Selfish Desires

Twenty times God described the promised land of Canaan as flowing with milk and honey. The word "flow" means to "gush out." God's promise to the Israelites was an overflowing of the very best. He wanted the Israelites to know they could dwell in Him and be completely satisfied.

Canaan was an attractive land, but the way to Canaan was difficult. Before the Israelites arrived in Canaan they had to cross the Jordan River. The word "Jordan" meant "to descend; to bring down; to subdue."

We all instinctively draw back from crossing Jordan. We prefer being lifted up to being brought down. But God's ways are higher than our ways. Before we can be

Spirit-led, we must be filled with the Holy Spirit by surrendering our right to being self-led.

1. Rom. 12:2 promises, "Then you will be able to test and approve what God's will is—his good, pleasing and perfect will." To whom was Paul speaking, and what did he say they needed to do? See Rom. 12:1.

2. To the Romans, the word "sacrifice" meant death. What do you think Paul meant by a "living sacrifice"? What has to die? What do we have to sacrifice before we can know God's good and perfect will?

3. Throughout the Old Testament, the victorious life is referred to as Canaan. Although the word "Canaan" means "to bend the knee" or "to humiliate," notice the glowing descriptions given of it in Num. 14:7-8 and Exod. 3:8.

4. In today's language the words "subdue," "humiliate," and "sacrifice" do not have appealing connotations. Neither was the Old Testament Tabernacle, covered with skins of animals, an appealing sight to onlookers. People who had never been inside might have wondered, "What do the Israelites think is so great about their place of worship? There's nothing attractive about animal skins." The beauty, though, was reserved for those who went inside. The bronze, gold, silver, burning incense, and constant supply of bread were beheld only by those who entered as worshipers. (The description of the Tabernacle and furnishings is in Exod. 25—30.)

The surrendered life is a life of rest, joy, and peace. But it comes only after an inward relinquishment to God's perfect will. Our selfish ambitions must be offered to God as a sacrifice.

Why do you think God requires us to offer ourselves as a sacrifice before we can know His will?

5. "I appeal to you therefore, brethren, and beg of you in view of [all] the mercies of God, to make a decisive dedication of your bodies—presenting all your members and faculties—as a living sacrifice, holy (devoted, consecrated) and well pleasing to God" (Rom. 12:1, AMP.).

Have you experienced that surrender to God? If you have not, would you write a heartfelt prayer of surrender, asking Him to give you His power so that all your desire will be to please Him?

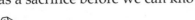

Nov 3

◆ Choose the Mind of Christ

The goal of spiritual formation is for Christ to be formed in us. Paul wrote, "My dear children, for whom I am again in the pains of childbirth until Christ is formed in you" (Gal. 4:19). When we choose to have the mind of Christ, to select what would please Him, Christ is being formed within us. In every new situation we want to be able to do as Paul did. He said, "I die daily" (1 Cor. 15:31, KJV).

1. "Let this mind be in you, which was also in Christ Jesus" (Phil. 2:5, KJV). What attitudes of Christ do verses 6-8 give?

2. What do these verses say about the attitudes we should *not* have in our lives?

3. Since we are to "let this mind be in [us]," we must make a deliberate choice—to speak and move only as Jesus would if He were in our situation. We choose to be no more anxious than He is. When a problem or relationship bothers us, we determine to please Him, ask Him for the mind of Christ, and expect Him to give us His thoughts, His love, His ideas for our situation. Do you want to have the mind of Christ in a conflict, situation, or problem? Tell Him that you prefer His attitudes to your own and that your strongest desire is to please Him.

I learned the principle of "If God is pleased, all is well" by considering Paul's declaration: "I resolved to know nothing while I was with you except Jesus Christ and him crucified" (1 Cor. 2:2). Paul said he had not focused on the Corinthians but on Christ. I began to examine my relationships by asking, "Is my primary concern in this relationship to know Christ's will and to please Him?"

As is usual after God gives an insight, He soon gave me opportunity to apply it. Someone difficult for me to appreciate entered my life. Although I did not show my irritation, I was tempted to feel it. Then the Lord reminded me that here was an opportunity to "know nothing . . . except Jesus Christ."

I quietly lifted my desire to the Lord: "Dear Lord, my only desire in this relationship is that You be pleased with my thoughts about her." God surprised me with plenty of grace to love her. She was no longer an irritation but a source of joy!

4. Look for small opportunities to show God you want to have the mind of Christ. George Watson, in his book *Soul Food*, writes that if we have a patient heart in small things—so small that no one but God notices—then surely our desire is to please only God.[2] Small things may simply mean we perform an unpleasant routine with joy. Perhaps we peacefully endure being contradicted, reproved, or slighted. We glorify God to a high degree when, for example, we seek to have Christ's attitude about the frustrating broken clothes dryer, or when we have a truly humble spirit about another receiving an honor we wanted. What does Luke 19:17 say about God's noticing details?

5. The Holy Spirit seeks to find places where God alone can be exalted. God wants to show himself to us and reveal His personal presence in the insignificant details of daily life. God alone knows when our joys are truly in pleasing Him and when we are willing for Him to have all the glory. Notice what the following verses say about God's knowledge of us.

 1 Sam. 2:3

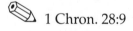 1 Chron. 28:9

 1 Thess. 2:4

6. Begin each day by reminding yourself that the key issue is gaining God's approval for your actions and attitudes. In what small ways can you show God your intentions to please Him today?

Pleasing God is more than doing the right activities. It's choosing the right attitudes. As we learn to respond with Christlike attitudes, we learn to have the mind of Christ. With this increased sensitivity, we'll become more aware of the Spirit's leadership in other areas.

7. In Phil. 2:1-4 Paul said their obedience would bring him joy. What attitudes does Paul mention in the following verses?

 verse 2

 verse 3

 verse 4

Elaine was having trouble obeying what she knew the Lord asked of her. Finally she said, "OK, Lord, in this one thing I'll obey You. I may never be able to do it again, but I will this one time." She determined to obey God by responding with a gracious, forgiving spirit in a difficult situation.

"At first it was not easy," she admitted, "but then I was surprised at the joy of obedience!"

8. Consider the insights from Phil. 2:1-4 as you look at the following situations. Write out what your attitudes will be if your focus is on the question "Is God pleased with my attitude?"

• My good deeds are unappreciated.

• My husband and I disagree about what to do on our vacation.

- My neighbor gets new carpet, but I can't afford to replace my worn rug.

Rees Howells founded a mission in which many were brought to Christ. After three years, Satan tempted Howells's coworker: "Unless you leave Rees Howells, you'll never be at your best. You need to have a work of your own."

When Howells learned what his coworker was thinking, the Lord said, "Why don't you give him the leadership of the mission? Be his intercessor."

For three years Howells had put all his time, money, and energies into the mission. Now that great prospects existed, God was asking him to step down and help his friend as his friend had helped him previously. The mission was growing, and as it would become more popular, people would naturally attribute all the success to his friend.

"It was a great inward conflict to allow my friend to get the outward success," Howells admitted. God was preparing him to find as much joy in a hidden life as in an open and successful one. Mr. Howells said he decided, "If my aim in life was to do God's will, then I could truly say either way would be equal joy."

God enabled him to love the man who took his place. "Build it as a great mission," Mr. Howells told his coworker. "The Lord will win souls through you, and I will be praying for you. I want the mission to become a greater success through you than it was through me."

We never learn the name of his coworker or what became of the mission, but Rees Howells's influence remains.[3]

9. The rewards of daily surrender are far greater than we realize they'll be before we sacrifice our personal desires to please God. What were the rewards for Jesus, according to Phil. 2:9-11?

We find the joy of the Lord in our obedience by praying, "Lord, I want to care only about pleasing You. Cleanse me from my own selfishness. Enable me to find more joy in Your approval than in having my own way."

Scriptural Role Model

God uses powerful word pictures in the Old Testament. We see Samuel sternly commanding Saul, "Now go, attack the Amalekites and totally destroy everything that belongs to them. Do not spare them; put to death men and women, children and infants, cattle and sheep, camels and donkeys" (1 Sam. 15:3).

Did Saul obey? "But Saul and the army spared Agag and the best of the sheep and cattle, the fat calves and lambs—everything that was good. These they were unwilling to destroy completely, but everything that was despised and weak they totally destroyed" (1 Sam. 15:9).

How like Saul we are prone to be! God asks us to totally destroy our desires for self, and we do away with most of them—enough to convince ourselves that we have obeyed. Had Samuel not come along and obeyed God by killing Agag, Agag would have caused great havoc. If we refuse to allow God to completely destroy sin, it will eventually destroy us.

Later, an Amalekite bragged to David that he had killed Saul (2 Sam. 1:9-10). The truth was that "Saul died because he was unfaithful to the LORD" (1 Chron. 10:13). Those who Saul was supposed to have destroyed reported his death happily.

Saul lost the kingdom and eventually his life because he refused to surrender to the Lord.

Memorize

"Yes, LORD, walking in the way of your laws, we wait for you; your name and renown are the desire of our hearts" (Isa. 26:8).

Prayer

Dear Lord, I admit that at times in my life I can't say, "My only desire is to please You." Cleanse me from any selfish desires that would motivate me to seek my own interests. You have promised to give the Holy Spirit to those who ask for Him. I ask now that the Holy Spirit would come into my life as a refining fire, a purifier of my unholy desires.

Purify my heart so that in each situation I can say, "I desire Your approval above all else." I trust You to fulfill Your promise, that if we confess our sins, You are faithful and just and will forgive us our sins and purify us from all unrighteousness. Thank You for providing all I need for life and godliness. In Jesus' name I pray. Amen.

4

WHEN FOLLOWING CHRIST MEANS SUBMITTING TO OTHERS

The followers of God know that real
freedom comes not when we do as we
please, but when we walk in the paths that
God has set for us.[1]
—*William Dyrness*

Introduction

During one period of her ministry, a faculty member of a
seminary worked under a supervisor who frequently sti-
fled her vision. She prayed much and thought surely God
would change her boss's mind, but He didn't.

"God wanted to form the image of Christ in me," she
later observed.

God first convinced her that He, God, was in charge of
the outcome of her work. She wasn't. Then He also taught
her that no one else controlled her ministry; God himself
was in control.

"I remember the rest of heart and the freedom that
came from knowing that God was in charge," she recalled.

She still had to look daily to the Spirit for power to
bless her boss, to pray for him, to speak well of him, and to
commend him. She soon recognized this daily choosing
the mind of Christ as the true spiritual discipline.

"What a service that man performed!" she exclaimed. She considered him to be one of the most influential people in her life, because he forced her to count on the Spirit's help to have a submissive spirit in a difficult situation.

Discussion and Questions

Often we want to joyfully follow the Lord, until following Him means submitting to another. Then suddenly we have a change of heart. We can determine the genuineness of our desire to follow God by our responses to those He places in our lives. If we are called to submit to an inflexible, uncaring authority, what might God want us to learn? What graces and gifts might He want to provide?

◆ Submission—Our Response to God

1. God has placed all of us under submission to another. What are some of the authority relationships mentioned in the following verses? Notice the frequent instruction to submit as though we're submitting to the Lord.

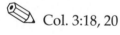 Col. 3:18, 20

 Eph. 5:21

 1 Pet. 2:13-14, 18-19

2. The controlling principle of submission in the New Testament is a response to Christ's love, rather than a response to the Law. What thoughts did Paul repeatedly use in the following verses as reasons we submit?

 Eph. 5:21-22

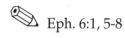 Eph. 6:1, 5-8

3. Submission seldom looks attractive unless we view it as our response to God. When we submit to the authority in our life in order to please God, we experience the joy of freedom. List several adjectives that would describe the differences in our attitude when we respond out of love for Christ rather than as an unpleasant duty.

4. How is the kingdom of God benefited when we submit as unto the Lord? See 1 Pet. 3:1 and Titus 2:9-10.

5. To submit to authority as unto the Lord, we must believe that God is in control. Paul understood that. "I, therefore, the prisoner of the Lord," Paul wrote in Eph. 4:1 (NKJV). The Romans had him in chains, but they didn't control him. Paul recognized the reality of this situation, and as a result, no bitterness tinged his words. Instead, with glorious freedom he declared, "I'm a prisoner of the Lord!"

How did Paul's perspective of his imprisonment affect his ability to write to the Ephesians? Would he have been able to write joyfully if he were holding a grudge against his authorities?

6. Moses would not take up his own quarrel when his brother and sister criticized him, so God stepped in. Read Num. 12:1-2. Consider the fact that God hears every word everyone speaks, whether it's directed to Him or not. In light of this, we don't need to be concerned with self-defense. If words spoken against us are not true and our spirit is meek, God will defend us. If those negative words are true, let's respond in the spirit of James 1:21.

7. Having a meek spirit does not mean we should never mention our concerns. It does mean, however, that when we do speak we depend upon God, not our words, to change the other person. "He must correct his opponents with courtesy and gentleness, in the hope that God may grant that they will repent and come to know the Truth" (2 Tim. 2:25, AMP.). Restate this verse in your own words. How does it apply to a present situation in your life?

8. When we want to correct someone, what often hinders our speaking with gentleness and faith in God?

Do we tend to see ourselves in control rather than God? Our faith, not our manipulation, enables the authority we have to hear God in our lives.

◆ God Leads the Submissive

We often neglect an obvious way to find God's will—submission. We can define submission as "trusting God to direct me through the authority put over me." This definition takes the focus off the authority and puts it on God. Our prayer becomes, "Lord, I'm submitting as unto You. I'm trusting You to guide me through the authority You've given me."

1. Read Rom. 13:1-7 and write down at least three insights God gives you regarding your authority and God.

  a.

  b.

  c.

2. Submission is a method both husbands and wives can use to determine God's will. When Paul says, "Submit to one another out of reverence for Christ" (Eph. 5:21), he is writing to both husbands and wives. If a decision is to be made and the wife has strong reservations, a wise husband remembers God's call for submission and unity. His desire to please God by having unity with his wife will protect him from forging ahead without her approval. Just as the wife is to trust God to direct her through her husband, the husband must trust God to direct him through a sense of oneness with his wife.

If our concern for unity reflects Christ's concern, we will seek unity before our personal desires. What do the following verses indicate about God's desire for unity in our relationships?

  1 Cor. 1:10

  Eph. 4:3

Phil. 2:2

3. On a talk show a woman presented her problem to a psychologist: "I'm in a no-win situation. My husband told me that I must either quit my job or it's all over between us. But when I'm not working, I'm just a slave. No one pitches in unless I demand some help. What should I do?"

"You must assert yourself," the psychologist advised. "It doesn't matter what your husband wants. Consider only what *you* want."

Following such advice doesn't allow Christ to be formed in us. If you were giving the woman advice from Phil. 2:5-11, what would you tell her?

4. How will the following scriptures help us keep in step with the Spirit when we need to be submissive? Write the implications the following verses could have for those who seek to know God's will regarding submission.

    a. "For promotion cometh neither from the east, nor from the west, nor from the south. But God is the judge: he putteth down one, and setteth up another" (Ps. 75:6-7, KJV).

    b. "He guards the course of the just and protects the way of his faithful ones" (Prov. 2:8).

c. "The king's heart is in the hand of the LORD; he directs it like a watercourse wherever he pleases" (Prov. 21:1).

d. "As the heavens are higher than the earth, so are my ways higher than your ways and my thoughts than your thoughts" (Isa. 55:9).

5. In the following illustrations, which of the above scriptures (or others) could be applied?
    a. Brenda was due a promotion at work, but her superior promoted a man instead of her.

b. Jody said her unsaved husband had asked her to quit some of her many church activities.

◆ The Responsibilities of the Submissive

Submission is not just blindly falling in step with another's wishes. Once when our children were young, my husband and I disagreed about how to spend the evening with our family. He wanted to spend the evening at home, but I thought it would be more profitable to take them across town to hear a special speaker.

"Oh, well—it's his responsibility; we'll just do whatever he wants," I recall thinking. The next morning I didn't feel right in my spirit about that decision. The Lord reminded me that I had failed to ask Him to direct the evening. I had ignored my part of the responsibility.

1. Queen Esther's spirit of submissiveness did not prevent her from convincing her husband that he was wrong. In Esther 4:15-16 notice what actions indicated that Esther's faith was in God, not just in her own efforts.

2. Esther didn't simply pray for her husband and say nothing. Notice that after she and her maids prayed, she could discern proper timing, appropriate methods, and right words. See Esther 5:1-8. What do you think might have happened if she had not sought the Lord before trying to change the king's mind? Do you think her seeking the Lord was more important in changing her or the king?

3. Superficially 1 Pet. 3:1 might appear to teach that we're never to say a word in our own defense. But, in fact, if we do not give our viewpoint, we're withholding from our authority. Can you think of situations in which it would be important to give an opposing opinion?

4. King Nebuchadnezzar commanded Daniel to eat rich, unclean foods and to drink wine, but Daniel felt this would be disobeying his God. Yet Daniel was able to peacefully resolve the issue. What indication does Dan. 1:9 give that Daniel had a good attitude?

5. God's solution may be to help us provide creative alternatives. But unless our attitudes are correct, we can seldom discern God's will in the situation. As a result of Daniel's maintaining a good spirit, he could recognize the real reason for the request. This gave him direction for a creative alternative. He understood what the king wanted and thought of a different way to accomplish the goal. See Dan. 1:11-14.

6. If we have an unkind or judgmental attitude when our authority asks us to do something wrong, what have we gained in God's sight? What attitudes should we display to others when we're trying to obey God? See James 3:17-18.

7. Can a wife use submission as an excuse to sin? Absolutely not. First Pet. 3:5-6 gives Sarah's submission as an example for other wives to follow. Yet in Gen. 20, Sarah's obedience to Abraham culminates in her harem residency. Does this prove that Christian wives should be in total, unqualified submission? Notice 1 Pet. 3:2. Who does Gen. 20:4-6 state that God was protecting?

Probably Peter uses Sarah as an example of submission referring to the general tenor of Sarah's life, not to one specific incident. Sarah's attitude of loving submission was apparent through her willing acceptance of a nomadic life. She had a calm and quiet spirit when following Abraham into the unknown. It is this submissive spirit Peter encourages wives to emulate.

Scriptural Role Model

Jesus "learned obedience from what he suffered" (Heb. 5:8). What suffering caused Jesus to learn obedience?

When Jesus was 12, He had to follow His parents "down to Nazareth" (Luke 2:51). Didn't they understand He was to be in His Father's house teaching? Surely they could see He was gifted! Why couldn't they realize what God wanted Him to do?

It must have been a form of suffering for Jesus to leave the Temple, where He was in His element teaching the Law to the astonished doctors, and return home to "do nothing" for 18 years. Yet Jesus learned His lesson of obedience well. He remained subject to His parents.

God is still teaching us through submission. As we give up our own ideas and submit one to another, we learn God's will.

Years later when Mary told Jesus of the need for more wine at the wedding in Cana, He replied, "Dear woman, why do you involve me? . . . My time has not yet come" (John 2:4).

Could it be that in His spirit Jesus sensed that His time for performing miracles had not come because He was still under Mary's authority? "Do whatever he tells you" (John 2:5), His mother told the servants, and with those words Mary put Jesus in charge. It's interesting that His time for public ministry did not come until His mother put others under His authority. Jesus had learned obedience by waiting for God's timing.

Even when submission is difficult, the lessons learned through obedience prepare us for service. Skipping those lessons yields a superficial preparation.

Memorize

"To the faithful you show yourself faithful, to the blameless you show yourself blameless" (Ps. 18:25).

Prayer

Dear Lord, please help me to remember that when I respond to others, You notice. You see if I'm guarding my attitude so You will be pleased. You notice if I'm trusting You to control my way. Teach me the freedom and joy of always responding to You. I pray this in Jesus' name. Amen.

5

"AM I COMMITTED TO OBEY?" QUIZ

I learned . . . the one vital principle of the
hearing heart, namely, that one must keep
in closest contact with him and be willing
to obey at any cost.[1]

—Hannah Hurnard

Introduction

"Dear Lord, why am I frequently defeated?" I prayed earnestly one night nearly 20 years ago. This prayer seemed to surface repeatedly in my earlier Christian life. As a teenager, I had trusted the Holy Spirit to come into my life, but where was the victory that was supposed to accompany the Spirit-filled life?

I recalled times when the Spirit had given me a gentle nudge: "Why not get out of bed early so you'll have time for prayer this morning?" or "Tell her why you're doing well on your job—you prayed about it." Too often I failed to follow through.

When I brought my confusion to the Lord, He very gently said to me, "Your heart is clean." What relief those words gave! Then He added what has become the desire of my heart: "But you need to learn to obey Me."

Learning this truth brought a new day in my spiritual life. I recognized that being spiritual meant being sensitive to the Holy Spirit.

A phrase from Gal. 6:1 in the *Amplified Bible* gives a similar definition: "You who are spiritual—who are responsive to and controlled by the Spirit."

But how do we become responsive to and controlled by the Holy Spirit? First, we set our goal to obey God. In this chapter we'll look at some questions to help us determine our commitment to obedience.

Discussion and Questions

1. *Can God count on me to fully obey?* God is pleased when He sees our efforts to obey. It's as though He says, "I see I can trust her. She wants to obey Me. I'll show her another thing I'd like her to do."

A friend of mine said that when she was in college someone told her, "Rather than asking God to direct you in the future, ask Him to help you love Him and His will with all your heart. If you love His will, He will see that you know it."

Have you ever thought, "If only I knew His will, I'd do it"? Who did Jesus say in John 7:17 would know His will? Why does God reveal His plans to those who meet this condition?

2. *Am I flexible, or do I want God to lead in a certain way?* George Mueller said that before he could discern God's will, he had to come to the point at which he wouldn't turn his hand over to change the outcome. Whatever God chose about the matter was fine with him.

Philip demonstrated this ability to let God choose when the Holy Spirit called him to leave a successful revival in Samaria and go to a desert to speak to one person (Acts 8:4-8, 26). We're prone to want to stick with what has worked in the past or continue doing what has given results.

A lot of people are trying to serve God in an advisory capacity. What are areas in which you tend to be inflexible?

3. *Am I obtaining all the information I can on the subject?* Those who are led by the Spirit do not put their minds in neutral. Sometimes, however, it would seem to be easier to be led by the Holy Spirit without bothering to prepare our minds.

To ask God for wisdom to guide us and then to fail to obtain all the information we can on the subject is like a farmer who asks for a crop without cultivating his land. We pray, learn all we can, and then believe He gives us the wisdom to make the best choice with our knowledge. One music minister said he and his wife realized that although they asked the Spirit to guide their song selections, they needed to enlarge their repertoire to provide the Holy Spirit more options.

Read the first phrase of 1 Pet. 1:13 and apply it to any situation in which you want God's guidance.

4. *Am I being led by integrity?* Would one decision be more honest or upright in any way? Would one choice be keeping a promise or fulfilling a scriptural command? How could Prov. 11:3 give practical help to someone seeking God's will? Consider what it means to have integrity.

5. *Am I seeking His will, or my own good?* We discern the Spirit's guidance when what we desire is to find the way we can best show God we love Him. If our prayer is "Lord, I want to know how to show You I love You in this situation," then He'll certainly show us His will. We're to seek God, not His gifts.

What did Jeremiah warn against in Jer. 45:5? Could this be a danger for us when we ask for God's guidance?

The more we love Christ and His will, the more our discernment increases. Read Phil. 1:9-10. Isn't this true also in a marriage? The more the husband and wife love each other, the more they try to understand and then do what pleases the other.

6. *Are my motives right, or do I want this for selfish purposes?* If our motives are pure, it means two things. First, it means that all our personal desires are second to God's will. Second, our motives are free from deceit.

It's so easy to make choices out of the desire to gain honor for ourselves. What danger did Jesus warn against in John 7:18?

"Do nothing out of selfish ambition" (Phil. 2:3). Is my primary concern building God's kingdom, or is it personal profit? If God's scrutiny reveals pride, we'll miss gaining the needed understanding. "With humility comes wisdom" (Prov. 11:2).

I was looking for recipes for Sunday dinner. "Dear Lord, help me find something to fix for guests," I prayed, and suddenly God had me looking at my motives. Did I want to impress them with my culinary skills? If so, God wasn't that concerned about helping me. He wanted to help me if I wanted to fix a good dinner for the right reasons. "What would be 'right' reasons?" I wondered. I didn't want to waste a lot of time sorting through recipes or cooking. I wanted the guests to enjoy the meal and feel loved by my preparations for them. When I could offer up to God those reasons for His help, I knew I could trust Him to help me.

Notice in 2 Chron. 32:31 that God tests our hearts. To those who humble themselves and seek only His will, no matter how He chooses, He promises wisdom.

7. *Am I rushing ahead, or am I cooperating with God's timing?* Repeatedly Jesus said, "My hour has not yet come" implying that nothing—His suffering, His friends, His enemies—could induce Him to rush ahead of God's timing. We cooperate with God when we act precisely in His timing.

David knew there should be a house of worship for the Lord, but the right time had not arrived. In the spirit of obedience, he made all the preparations but left the work to his son Solomon. Those who are responsive and sensitive to the Holy Spirit will find that God's timing is perfect for the situation. According to Eccles. 3:1-8, what are some of the things God says are important to do at the right time?

8. *Have I trained myself to look to Him prayerfully on a moment-by-moment basis?* If we always lift our moments of perplexity to Him, we discover that He's willing to direct every detail of our lives. "In him we live and move and have our being" (Acts 17:28). We make no move, say no words, without His knowing it.

Often our greatest regrets result from simply failing to seek Him in all things—even when we think the answer is obvious. Satan often tries to deceive us by making the wrong decision seem so correct that we don't need to ask for God's guidance. What factors do you think caused Joshua's failure in Josh. 9:3-15? How can these serve as warnings to us?

The answer seemed obvious. Common sense told them what to do. We don't know if they forgot to inquire of the Lord or if the idea to inquire came and they rejected it. Perhaps it doesn't matter. We are responsible to bring our decisions before Him. Satan's plans are often so subtle that we think we're obeying God while choosing our own way.

The habit of always praying before deciding is the key to constant obedience. Often we forget, we don't see the need, or maybe we're afraid of the answer. We have not, because we ask not.

Everything should be the subject of prayer, not necessarily of prolonged prayer, but of a momentary call to God for help. Maybe such attentiveness to prayer seems impossible, but it is a habit we gain through perseverance. God has made it clear that nothing that concerns His children is too trivial to be mentioned.

9. *Am I hindered from finding God's will because of past disobedience?* Disobedience leads us out of light and into darkness. If we fail to sense His leadership frequently, it could be that He has asked us to obey, and we haven't. Go back to the last time you acknowledged His leadership, and ask Him to teach you any point of disobedience since that time.

10. *Am I becoming more equipped to discover God's will by walking in all the light I've been given?*

Continued obedience brightens our way. In the early morning when the light first comes through the window in our bedroom, we can see only the outline of furniture. By midday we can see a pin on the floor. The longer we walk in God's light the more light He gives and the more we'll understand His precise wishes. What is the promise of Prov. 4:18?

At one point in C. S. Lewis's Chronicles of Narnia, the children were lost. Only one of the children wanted to follow Aslan, the godlike character in the story. At first she could hardly see Aslan, but she followed what she believed to be the lion. The longer she followed him, the clearer he became to her and to the other children. As we continue to follow the Holy Spirit, He becomes more real and His will plainer.

According to Heb. 5:14, the mature can distinguish between good and evil. How have they gained that ability?

11. *Am I faithful to my routine?* God leads as we walk in the path of duty. We find God's plans for our future as we daily fulfill our obligations out of love for the Lord.

What are some of your duties today? Write a term paper, do laundry, care for preschoolers, teach biology? God expects us to be faithful in our routine responsibilities. "Since we live by the Spirit, let us keep in step with the Spirit" (Gal. 5:25). To keep in step with the Spirit, you will be faithful in all you have to do. What will faithfulness to your routine include today?

When we want a special message from God's Word, how do we know where to read? Usually we find it when we read where our routine says to read, expecting the Lord to give us what we need in that passage.

One morning I wanted God's blessing in a certain situation and wondered if I should fast breakfast and lunch. I knew the Spirit would lead me. As our daughter read Ps. 37 in that morning's family devotions, I took the phrase "Wait on the LORD" (v. 34, KJV) as my answer. I would fast to tell the Lord I was waiting on Him.

The next morning I opened to Isaiah. "I really haven't been getting much out of these chapters," I thought and was tempted to skip to another book. But I stuck with it. When I came to Isa. 25:9, I knew God had this special promise there for me that day: "Lo, this is our God; we have waited for him, and he will save us: this is the LORD; we have waited for him, we will be glad and rejoice in his salvation" (KJV).

12. *Am I leaning on my own understanding, rather than depending upon the Holy Spirit?* Jesus looked to His Father, not to His own intellect, to know what to say. Notice His words in John 14:10. If we're Spirit-led, should we be able to give a similar testimony?

13. *Am I moving in the direction I think the Lord would have me go?* Abraham's servant successfully found a wife for Isaac, because he was able to say, "I being in the way [of obedience and faith] the Lord led me" (Gen. 24:27, AMP.). The Lord led him as he started in the direction he thought was right.

Often we must take the first step in the direction we think the Lord is leading, before we can discern a second step. God's Word "is a lamp to [our] feet" (Ps. 119:105). A lamp for our feet gives light only for a short distance. Why do you think God waits until we're moving in the correct direction to give us guidance?

Scriptural Role Model

Once when the disciples went fishing, they caught nothing. Early the next morning Jesus stood on the shore and said, "Friends, have you any fish?"

"No," they replied.

So He told them, "Throw your net on the right side of the boat, and you will find some."

At this point, they didn't recognize Jesus by His voice or by the directions He gave. They needed to obey before they knew it was the Lord. When they obeyed, they were unable to haul the net in because of the large number of fish.

Then John said to Peter, "It is the Lord."

Jesus' voice still comes over the wind and waves of life, and often we won't know until later that it was He. But as His disciples who want to obey His voice, we learn to respond to the impulses. Later we'll know.

Memorize

"I will instruct you and teach you in the way you should go; I will counsel you and watch over you" (Ps. 32:8).

Prayer

Dear Lord, if only I could grasp how You delight in my obedience, I would shun every temptation to want my own way instead of Yours. I long to live in Your presence every day, to receive all I say and do from the Father, as Jesus did. Thank You for Your promise to guide me continuously. Teach me to always respond quickly to Your will. In Jesus' name I pray. Amen.

6

LEARNING TO FOLLOW THE HOLY SPIRIT

When you have developed a listening ear, it does not take a loud voice or a jolting event to guide you. It becomes natural to you to expect suggestions or restraints from the Spirit. Your life almost unconsciously becomes prayer without ceasing and guidance without ceasing.[1]

—Wesley Duewel

Introduction

A frequent term used to describe the Spirit's coming to us is "poured." What an active term! I had thought that the Holy Spirit fills us much as my mother filled a jar with tomatoes, sealed it, and set it away to be preserved. But the Holy Spirit is being continually poured out on those who obey. Jesus, who always obeyed the Father, had the Spirit poured on Him without measure (John 3:34).

The picture of our being filled with the Holy Spirit is more like a sailboat that is being blown along by the wind. As long as faith and obedience hold open our sails, the Holy Spirit controls us. When we turn our sails away from His voice, we are no longer Spirit-controlled.

Discussion and Questions

"Since we live by the Spirit, let us keep in step with the Spirit" (Gal. 5:25). The Holy Spirit leads us as we remain constantly tuned to His guidance, His impulses, His hesitancies. Moses discovered the secret of being Spirit-led. He constantly "saw him who is invisible" (Heb. 11:27).

As we keep our eyes on Jesus, we'll be among those "who are spiritual—who are responsive to and controlled by the Spirit" (Gal. 6:1, AMP.). In this chapter we'll examine ways to identify the Spirit.

1. *Expect His guidance to be natural.* Rarely does God give dramatic guidance. If we are looking to God, we can safely believe He is guiding us through our natural inclinations. God designed that the judging powers He has given us should ordinarily furnish the basis for our decisions. We can be relaxed, yet open and alert to any suggestion as we look to the Lord to give us wisdom. The more intimate our relationship with the Holy Spirit, the more natural we become, the more we become "ourselves." We are to be free to be ourselves while trusting God to guide us.

Notice how the following verses from Proverbs suggest that the righteous naturally know what is right to do and to say.

10:32

14:6

14:33

16:23

2. *The Spirit often gives counsel through others.* What do the following verses in Proverbs say about God using the comments or insight of others to guide us?

 15:22

 24:6

 27:17

3. *Expect God to guide by putting desires into your heart.*
  a. When we seriously seek God's will about something, we can often discern what He wants by our strong desires. What does He promise to give us if we delight ourselves in Him and His Word? See Ps. 37:4.

  b. What dangers might there be in following our own desires? How can we guard against these dangers?

  c. We can easily ignore these inward impressions or desires implanted by the Holy Spirit. In 1 Kings 17:7-12, God commanded the widow of Zarephath to care for Elijah. Notice in verse 9 what God told Elijah about the widow.

d. It appears that the widow did not know she had been commanded by God to feed Elijah. Her only clue to her assignment was the little tug at her heart to respond to Elijah's need when he showed up in her village. She saw someone in need and had enough compassion to meet that need. Could it be that we have been commanded by God to provide for someone, and He wants to tell us this by implanting within us a desire to help? What clues might God give us to help us discover those He expects us to assist?

Despite having a Spirit-implanted desire, we may experience fear. One day Patty called, saying, "I think the Holy Spirit wants me to visit Larry. Please pray. I'm afraid to go."

Both she and Larry attended our home Bible study, and Larry was now in the hospital with cancer. We weren't sure he had made a commitment to the Lord. Later, Larry's wife said, "Patty came into the room, and as we made small talk, I wondered why she was staying so long. Finally she began telling how the Lord had delivered her from dealing drugs. The Holy Spirit used her testimony as a turning point for Larry's faith."

4. *God's voice may be an idea springing from our hearts and registering in our minds as a spontaneous thought.* Often recognizing the Spirit is as simple as hearing the spontaneous thoughts that remind us, "You haven't prayed today," or "She needs a word of encouragement."

Many of the spontaneous thoughts given by the Holy Spirit will be guidance for the sake of others. When we live like Jesus, we live for others. He will give us ideas of ways we can pour out His love in practical ways.

Have you had spontaneous thoughts giving you ideas of ways to apply such verses as Gal. 6:2?

5. *Expect the providences of God and His promptings to harmonize.* Often providences (circumstances that appear to be arranged by God) interpret His will.

  a. Paul planned and wanted to go to Rome, but the Lord kept closing the door. We are to try all that our heart says to do, trusting the Lord to block us if it's not His will. How could Prov. 16:9 apply to this?

  b. Providences in themselves are inadequate and can be confusing. If Joseph had taken his being sold into slavery and imprisonment as indications that he was out of God's will, he would have misread providence. God was using circumstances to develop Joseph's character and to prepare him to become a leader. What was Joseph later able to look back and say? See Gen. 50:20.

  c. God often *confirms* His will through providential circumstances, but we must use those as only a secondary source of guidance. The Holy Spirit is our Guide, not circumstances. Can you think of a time when the Holy Spirit confirmed His will for you through circumstances? Or a time when you were led astray by what appeared to be providential circumstances?

6. *Notice what gifts you have.*

   a. Natural skills are often an indication of God's will for us. Wouldn't we expect a loving Creator to coordinate our skills with His plans for us? How does Exod. 31:3 indicate that the Holy Spirit selects the gifts He gives us because He wants them used for His purposes?

   b. What are some of the things you enjoy doing that might indicate what God wants you to do?

7. *Determine if a gentle or demanding spirit is leading.*

   a. Christ leads us with patience and with tenderness, compelling us by love. "O love that will not let me go" is a phrase from a song that speaks of a drawing, not a driving, force. Love is the compelling motivator of God. If the Holy Spirit is leading, we don't feel pressured but are allowed time to reflect. See John 10:3-4 and consider what it means to be *led* rather than *driven*. What words would you use to describe each?

   b. If a "leading" is of God, the way will always open for us to obey it. Who goes before us, according to John 10:4?

   c. Notice the expression "he goes on ahead" in John 10:4. Jesus goes before us to open a way, and we are to follow in His steps. If Jesus is leading, we never need to insist on opening our own way. Riding roughshod over opposition usually is an indication that we're not walking in the Spirit. If the Lord goes before us, He will open doors, and we won't need to batter down barriers. Our spirits will be gentle, also, as we imitate the Spirit of God.

One night during devotions when I was living in a Bible school dorm, a strong insistent voice began throwing accusations into my mind. I was so troubled that the next morning I told a teacher about the experience. She wisely counseled me concerning the difference between an impression from Satan and one from the Lord. "Often Satan will come with force," she cautioned, "but that's not God's way. Jesus' leading is always gentle. You can recognize Him, because He does not force or coerce, but kindly speaks."

8. *Reject the spirit of fear.* As I drove to a bridal shower, I prayed for the Spirit's leadership. What could I say in this group of women who were mostly strangers? I recalled that God does not give a spirit of fear, so self-consciousness would be an indication that I was not being Spirit-directed. A spirit of fear would tell me I wasn't "abiding."

By remembering this, I was more aware of responding to the Spirit. To the degree that we respond to the Spirit, to that degree we are free to be ourselves and to have quiet spirits. Where the Spirit of the Lord is, there is liberty, which includes the liberty to be at ease. What kind of spirit does God give? See 2 Tim. 1:7. What might be some of the clues that we are not led by the Holy Spirit?

9. *Expect the Spirit to have us put people before projects.* Why did Paul not take an open door in Troas? See 2 Cor. 2:12-13.

Paul's care and concern for his friend Titus went beyond his desire to enter every open door. He considered his relationship to Titus more important than preaching Christ's gospel. Understanding the priorities God wants us to have is a great source of help in obtaining the Holy Spirit's guidance. Why do you think the Holy Spirit leads us to place relationships above projects?

10. *The Spirit gives appropriate attitudes.* It is never God's will for us to say unkind things or do thoughtless, unloving acts. Often following the Spirit is making a conscious choice to "Let this mind be in [us], which was also in Christ Jesus" (Phil. 2:5, KJV). Being divinely led is not simply being directed to do the right activities; it's having the right attitudes. As we learn to respond with Christlike attitudes, we're learning to have the mind of Christ.

"A divinely led person will be characterized by the utmost decency, propriety and true courteousness."[2] First Cor. 13:4-7 will be true in our lives when we're obedient to the Spirit. Using these verses, describe our attitude when we are led by the Spirit.

As you read Gal. 5:22-23, consider how consciously choosing these attitudes to be in our lives invites the Spirit to be in control.

11. *The Holy Spirit is a God of order.* The first activity of the Spirit mentioned in Scripture was to bring order out of chaos. See Gen. 1:2. What are some of the different ways the Spirit does that for us today?

12. *The Holy Spirit may guide by giving a sense of restraint.* See Acts 16:6-7 for an example of this.

George Mueller said, "The stops of a good man, as well as his steps, are ordered by the Lord."[3] Divine approval to go ahead and divine restraint are equally important. Notice in Num. 9:18 that God provided both for the children of Israel.

The Spirit may give us an inner hesitancy, causing us to not say or write statements we would later regret. He may restrain us from making unwise financial decisions. He may restrain us from praying a prayer that is not in His will, as He did for Paul in 2 Cor. 12:7-9. Can you recall any restraints the Lord has placed upon you?

When we obey this inner hesitancy, we have an abiding sense of peace. Guidance can be as simple as avoiding what robs us of God's peace. See Phil. 4:7.

Scriptural Role Model

Long before Baby Jesus was born, God prophesied that a king would be born in Bethlehem. God's plans caused Caesar Augustus to issue a decree that all the world should be taxed.

Mary and Joseph arrived in Bethlehem confident that their Heavenly Father was taking care of every detail—but there was no room for them or for Baby Jesus in the inn. Mary may have been tempted to doubt the divine planning. Surely there would have been arrangements made for Jesus to be born in a respectable place!

Sometimes we think God must have forgotten to plan some details of our lives. Things don't seem to fall together. But God always provides, although not always in the way we anticipate. Sometimes He says, "I have higher purposes than simply allowing all to fall together easily. Trust Me to be your loving Guide no matter how things seem."

Memorize

"I will put my spirit within you, and cause you to walk in my statutes, and ye shall keep my judgments, and do them" (Ezek. 36:27, KJV).

Prayer

Dear Lord, You love me better than I love myself. Even without knowing all Your plans and purposes for me, I love them above my own desires. Teach me to always wait for You, to always walk in the Spirit. Thank You for Your promise never to leave me nor forsake me. In Jesus' name. Amen.

7

WHAT IF I'VE FAILED TO FOLLOW?

Do not be too cast down when you have reason to believe that you have missed the Holy Spirit's signal. If the Holy Spirit has been grieved, He will let you know in a gentle chiding. . . . It is the devil who cracks the whip, not God.[1]

—Richard S. Taylor

Introduction

"I don't have trouble praising God and believing He is in control in all situations—except when I've messed up," a friend commented. "When the problems were caused by my own failures, then I wonder if the Lord wants to help me."

His comment reminded me of a dark time in my life when I was under a cloud because of a failure. "How can I expect Him to have mercy on me again?" I wondered.

Then I discovered Ps. 147:11—"The LORD delights in those . . . who put their hope in his unfailing love." What good news it was to learn that God took pleasure in me if I hoped in His mercy! He didn't want me to doubt His willingness to forgive.

Any of us can make a mistake and miss God's will in some decision or action, but our God is loving, merciful, and understanding! "As a father has compassion on his children, so the LORD has compassion on those who fear him; for he knows how we are formed, he remembers that we are dust" (Ps. 103:13-14).

Are you defeated by discouragement due to past failures to obey His will? In *Let God Guide You Daily*, Wesley Duewel writes:

> No mistake is so serious but that God can start anew and make something worthwhile from your life. It is said that in making a Persian rug the master weaver stands on one side of the loom and shouts instructions to the small boys weaving on the other side. If a boy should make a serious mistake, a truly great master weaver can weave the boy's error into the pattern and others will never realize a mistake was made. God is far greater than any master weaver. God can take any surrendered life and even weave our mistakes into something useful and beautiful.[2]

Discussion and Questions

Jesus didn't chide the disciples after they failed to watch with Him for one hour in the Garden of Gethsemane. Although He encouraged them when the opportunity was available, He never mentioned it again to them. Instead, He turned their attention to what was ahead, saying, "Rise, let us go!" (Matt. 26:46).

This appears to be the pattern of how God deals with His people. Before they fail, He warns sternly against sin and failure. Afterward, though, He says, "Let's look ahead—not back!" He never delights in reminding us of past failures. The accuser, Satan, would have us focus on those, but not our loving Lord. Instead, He can reshape our mistakes so that they look as though they were part of His plan. Our part is to trust God. The moment we trust Him to take over in our situation, it's all over for Satan.

Let's look at the proper attitude to have if we've failed, and then, to prevent future disobedience, consider attitudes that may have caused our failures.

◆ What if We've Failed?

"If only I had said something differently!" I wrote in my journal one morning. "Why, Lord? Why do I have to keep learning the same lesson?" After prayer—feeling that I was on the trash heap but trying to praise the Lord anyway—I began preparing breakfast. The psalmist's phrase "Hope thou in God: for I shall yet praise him" (Ps. 42:11, KJV) came to me. As I realized that through faith David saw future cause for rejoicing, my "if onlys" disappeared.

1. God is pleased if we accept His mercy. Sometimes we think of God as reluctant to forgive us when we mess up and have to come asking forgiveness, but what is happening in heaven when we ask for mercy? See Luke 15:7, 10, 32.

2. Why do you think this is true? Read Ps. 33:18 and 147:11.

3. Think of times you've asked God for forgiveness. Write Him words of thanks for His rejoicing as He forgave you.

4. If we've done something with a clear conscience and later see that we did the wrong thing, we can trust God to protect us from ill effects. What had Abimelech done wrong, and why did God excuse him, according to Gen. 20:5-6?

Phoebe Palmer, in *The Promise of the Father*, wrote of receiving an impression to speak a word for the Lord. She hesitated, deciding to pray about it first. She went away to pray, and just as she bowed to pray, the Holy Spirit whispered, "Did you not this morning ask to be filled with the knowledge of the will of God? Why then did you not do that which was in your heart, knowing that the Lord was with you?"

She saw her error and hurried back to speak, but her opportunity was gone. She wrote, "I felt ashamed before the Lord; but I felt my heavenly Father did not condemn me, for He saw that my intention was to please him."[3]

5. Has Satan ever told you, "You've failed, so God isn't interested in helping you"? In the story of the Gibeonite deception (in Josh. 9:3-15), Joshua failed to seek God's guidance. Because of this failure, he had to fight a battle he would not have had to fight. See Josh. 10:1-14. Did God say, "You're on your own now—this battle is your fault, so I'm going to let you handle it"? See Josh. 10:6-8.

6. What was the miracle God performed for the Israelites in this battle? See verses 13-14.

7. Past times of disobedience need not make us give up in defeat. God can still use us. Even though Joshua was misled and made a treaty with the Gibeonites, he didn't despair. He made the deceivers submit to him. See Josh. 9:23.

8. The psalmist assures us of God's constant presence and writes that God has "beset me behind and before" (Ps. 139:5, KJV). God goes behind us, much as a mother goes behind her child, picking up what is dropped and trying to undo the effects of the child's mistakes. Even if the mistake has been the child's fault, the mother is still willing and eager to help.

Even when our children are older and we fear we've failed them, we can commit them to God with confidence. "Dear Lord, go behind me—bring my family into Your presence despite my failures," we can pray; and God, who is "behind us," makes all things, even our failures, work together for good if we trust Him.

What does God promise in Phil. 4:19? What needs might we have if we feel we've failed?

A friend once showed artist John Ruskin an expensive handkerchief on which a blot of ink had left an ugly mark.

"Nothing can be done with this now," said the friend, preparing to discard it.

Ruskin asked if he could have the handkerchief. He later returned it to his friend, who was amazed when he saw it. With India ink, the artist had drawn a unique design, using the ugly blot as the focus for his creation. What had once appeared worthless was now a treasured work of beauty.[4]

9. When disobedience occurs, it is a great comfort to remember that God's mercies are new each morning. God is much more merciful than we let ourselves believe. God can overrule our failures or mistakes. Have you wasted years because of failure? What is the promise in the first phrase of Joel 2:25?

10. God's plans are not static. If we've failed, we find that He is a God of multiple plans for us. See Ps. 40:5 and Jer. 29:11. Notice that the word "plans" in Jer. 29:11 is in the plural. He has plans for our spiritual life, finances, home life, employment—*all* our needs. God is a God who plans for every contingency.

◆ Learning from Past Failures

Sometimes to get beyond past failures, we need to look carefully at the reasons for our errors. In fact, we can often profit from past mistakes by looking carefully at the reasons we've failed. Although the Holy Spirit doesn't chide us unmercifully, He often uses our failures to help us in future situations, if we thoughtfully and prayerfully reflect upon them. Allow the Holy Spirit to help you identify indicators of a disobedient spirit.

1. *Delayed obedience.* Delay is often an indication of an unwilling spirit. We don't say, "No, I won't do it," for that would be unacceptable, but we find an excuse to delay obedience. In Deut. 1:19-22, the Israelites delayed obedience of what they knew they were to do. What did the psalmist say in Ps. 119:60? Why is it important to obey quickly?

Catherine Marshall told how the Holy Spirit used a failure of hers to teach her. One night when she was alone, close to midnight there came a loud knocking on the door. She asked who it was and heard the voice of an acquaintance whose sister was dying of cancer.

She opened the door, and the lady asked Catherine to drive her to pray at her sister's bedside. She had not telephoned the sick woman's husband to tell him of this nocturnal visit, so Catherine demurred, asking if she could go to the bedside the following day. Reluctantly, her visitor agreed and left. But when they reached her sister the following morning, the sick woman had sunk into a deep coma, and she died later that day.

Catherine said the Spirit put His finger where it hurt: "Not enough flexibility or promptness in obeying Me. So you drive to another town in the middle of the night. Forget sleep. Forget your convenience. Even ignore certain amenities, as you see them. When I say 'Go,' I'll take care of the amenities too."[5]

2. *Complaining spirit.* A complaining spirit, a frequent cause of the Israelites' failures, may also be a cover-up for a rebellious, disobedient spirit. Notice carefully in Num. 17:5 and 10 who God said the people were complaining against. What does this say about the importance of not complaining?

What things are you most prone to complain about? In what ways might your complaints be against God?

3. *Defensive attitude.* Sometimes we make mistakes (such as having a wrong spirit) because we rely upon our own ability to defend ourselves, rather than upon God. Notice that according to Ps. 37:5-6 we don't need to defend ourselves.

4. *Independent spirit.* Most people, even many Christians, are satisfied with man's natural wisdom, but we must be determined to go beyond that. When we depend upon the Spirit for our words, we are enabled to better express our thoughts—yet our individuality is not destroyed. Notice in 1 Cor. 2:13 that Paul was not content to speak words taught him by human wisdom.

5. *Unwillingness to take a risk.* Caleb didn't make the same mistake that his fellow Israelites did. He was so eager to obey God that he was willing to face uncertainty when others refused. See Num. 13:30-31. What rewards did God give to Caleb in Num. 14:24?

6. *Self-assertion.* The desire for recognition slips in so subtly if we don't guard against seeking our own glory rather than God's. Although Paul loved the Thessalonians enough to share his life with them (see 1 Thess. 2:8), notice that his focus wasn't on trying to please them. See 1 Thess. 2:4-6.

7. *Wrong motives.* God is more concerned about why we do something than about what we do. One time after I realized that I had missed the Lord's will in a matter, I wanted to learn the cause of my mistake, so I began writing out the details of the episode. At one point the Holy Spirit allowed me to see that my motive had been to impress. Instantly I realized why Satan had been able to lead me astray. We lose the ability to discern correctly when pride, selfishness, or any other wrong attitude is the underlying reason for our actions. What wrong motives does Phil. 2:3 warn against? Why do you think God is so concerned about our motives?

8. *Lack of faith.* When Moses disobeyed the Lord by striking the rock instead of speaking to it, we might say he was impatient or stressed. What did God say about it? See Num. 20:12.

Notice that in Heb. 3:18-19 God interchanges the words "unbelief" and "disobedience." Why are those two words interchangeable?

If you are troubled about a failure in the past, write out each detail, trusting the Lord to teach you anything He wants you to learn from the situation. Then hear His words—"Rise, let us go!"—and don't look back. Trust Him to bring good to you from this point regarding this situation.

Scriptural Role Model

In Neh. 8, the Levites read from the book of the Law of God, and the people wept as they saw their sins. Nehemiah instructed them, "Do not grieve, for the joy of the LORD is your strength" (Neh. 8:10). Notice that Nehemiah didn't say, "Keep repenting for your sins." Repentance is appropriate, but once we've expressed a repentant spirit, we are to rejoice in God's mercy. We gain strength as we rejoice!

Memorize

"Like as a father pitieth his children, so the LORD pitieth them that fear him. For he knoweth our frame; he remembereth that we are dust" (Ps. 103:13-14, KJV).

Prayer

Thank You, Lord, for delighting in me simply because I hope in Your mercy instead of doubt Your love. Because of Your mercy, You don't reward evil for evil but love me with an everlasting love. Help me to focus on Your mercies that never fail.

I'm trusting You to go behind me and bring good from the situations in which I've failed. You are also going before me, making the crooked places straight. How I love following You! I pray this in Jesus' name. Amen.

8

METHODS OF LISTENING TO THE LEADER

In much of our prayer there is really little
thought of God. Our mind is taken up with
the thought of what we need and not with the
loving Father of whom we are seeking it. We
should look to the Holy Spirit to lead us into
the presence of God, and should not be hasty
in words until He has brought us there.[1]
—R. A. Torrey

Introduction

Since the beginning of time, God has sought to commune with us. The Lord walked in the garden, offering intimate fellowship with Adam and Eve. After their fellowship ended, God again sought man's communion by offering His voice to the children of Israel (in Deut. 5:22-31).

When Moses told the Israelites that God's voice came with fire (the symbol of purging and purification), rather than welcoming an opportunity to hear God's voice, they came up with an alternative plan.

"Moses," the Israelites said, "why don't you 'go near and listen to all that the LORD our God says. Then tell us whatever the LORD our God tells you' [v. 27]." "Rather than enjoying a face-to-face relationship with God as Moses did, they were content with a list of laws to live by."[2]

We, too, are faced with these two alternatives. Either we will accept living in communion with Him, which means we also accept coming into the cleansing flame of His holy presence, or we will live by the Law.

Either we are led by the Spirit, or we live by a list of rules. "If you are led by the Spirit, you are not under law" (Gal. 5:18), yet as we keep in step with the Spirit, we will spontaneously keep the demands of the Law. How much more wonderful it is to submit to God and to live by the Spirit than to live by a list of rules!

The writer to the Hebrews reminds us of the Israelites' fear at the fiery mountain and warns, "See to it that you do not refuse him who speaks" (12:25). God is still speaking, offering us His fellowship. Will we accept His voice and the fire that accompanies it?

Discussion and Questions

At times it might appear easier to live by a list of rules than to learn a moment-by-moment submission to His voice. We must pay a price to hear God's voice, but the rewards are far greater than we realize. How can we learn to follow the Spirit rather than rules or traditions? We'll look at two ways we can attempt to hear God's voice.

◆ Interactive Reading

Interactive reading, or meditative reading, is viewing Scripture from every angle, turning it over in our minds in order to hear God. We are holding the Scripture in the light of His presence, waiting for Him to explain it to us.

George Mueller said that until he discovered that the most important thing he had to do was to listen to God speak through the Word, his mind often wandered for the first 15 to 30 minutes of his devotions. After this discovery, he began to ask the Lord's blessing upon His Word. Then he searched every verse—not for the sake of finding something to share with others, but for the sake of finding God's personal message to him.

Such attentive listening requires us to focus our whole attention, expecting to interact with the words. When we read other books we may question the text, but when we read God's Word we allow the text to question us.

1. What do the following verses declare that the Word does in our lives?

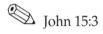 John 15:3

 2 Tim. 3:16-17

 Heb. 4:12

 James 1:22-25

2. To develop Bible reading methods appropriate for you, follow the desire of your heart—which will probably also be the suggestion of the Spirit. The following suggestions may help you to listen attentively to God when reading the Bible:

- Read in a quiet place, if possible.
- Redirect your thoughts to be centered on God's Word.
- Focus on God, who is within your spirit, and expect to hear Him speak. "For God does speak—now one way, now another—though man may not perceive it" (Job 33:14).
- Pray that you will be open to God's Spirit. Sometimes the "eyes of our hearts" become glazed over, and we

need to pray Paul's prayer for ourselves. What did he pray in Eph. 1:18?

• Read as though the Word is God's audible voice speaking.

3. Which of these suggestions do you regularly follow? Which would you like to put into practice in the coming days?

4. Watch for ideas that catch your interest. Your objective is not to read a certain amount of verses or to analyze all the meanings of the text. If you are particularly struck by what one verse says, take time to let God speak to you through that verse. Ponder it in your mind. What are we promised if we meditate?

 Josh. 1:8

 Ps. 119:98-100

 Ps. 1:2-3

5. Rewrite 1 Tim. 4:15, applying it to your approach to Scripture.

Although my dad was a farmer, when he was a young man he occasionally helped out as a lay preacher. In one service at which he was to speak, he put money into the offering, unaware that it would be given to him. At the close of the service someone handed him the offering with the comment, "If you had put more into it, you would have gotten more out of it."

I thought of that comment during an early morning Bible reading, and I decided to put more into it. I began memorizing the first few verses of 2 Corinthians.

At first I didn't find much for application, but I continued to memorize the verses as I had been taught to memorize piano music—repeating each phrase six times by memory, always including the beginning of the next phrase.

While saying the words I let them filter through my thoughts. Did they give any direction or any promise for today? Paul instructed Timothy: "Meditate upon these things; give thyself wholly to them" (1 Tim. 4:15, KJV). I tried to set my mind to gain understanding and to give myself wholly to the words.

Suddenly I understood how one phrase applied to me. As always when my search is rewarded, I realized that I was indebted to my Guide. "Flesh and blood hath not revealed it unto thee, but my Father which is in heaven" (Matt. 16:17, KJV).

6. It is important for us to reflect on Scripture so the Lord will give us understanding (knowledge of how to put His Word into practice). What happens if we fail to understand the Word because we have not reflected on it? See Matt. 13:19.

7. Oswald Smith said that to be filled with the Word is the same as being filled with the Spirit. Having a desire to be filled with the Word is only a step away from having a desire to memorize. We notice previously overlooked details of

Scripture when we commit God's Word to memory. What phrases in the following verses might refer to memorizing?

 Prov. 2:1

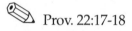 Prov. 22:17-18

8. God told Moses to teach the people His words in a song "because it will not be forgotten by their descendants" (Deut. 31:21). Set your favorite verses to a familiar tune. Sing them during your devotions, while you do the dishes, while you ride in the car. Both you and your children will own them forever. Which verse will you set to music?

◆ Two-way Prayer

Speaking

1. Successful praying is "'not by might nor by power, but by my Spirit,' says the LORD Almighty" (Zech. 4:6). What is the role of the Spirit in our praying, according to Eph. 2:18 and 6:18?

2. We can trust God to give us the Spirit of prayer if we ask Him. Claim His promise in Luke 11:9-13.

3. "But you, dear friends, . . . pray in the Holy Spirit" (Jude 20). The Holy Spirit helps us in at least three ways to pray:

    a. The Spirit gives us a desire or an inclination to pray. Sometimes He does this by helping us see a need or by bringing to our mind someone who needs prayer. What an honor it is when the Spirit gives us a hunger to pray for someone! Have you ever felt drawn to pray for someone and later learned that he or she was in need?

    The Holy Spirit often impresses us to pray for those for whom we regularly pray. Wesley Duewel wrote, "One of my prayer lists names fifty-four persons who are imprisoned for Christ. I try to name each one briefly before the Lord daily. At times as I awakened in the morning, one of those names was instantly on my heart; it was God's special assignment for that day. Sometimes God may bring to your mind someone you have not thought of for months; accept that one as your prayer assignment that day."[3]

    b. The Holy Spirit teaches us what to pray. Our goal in prayer is not so much to tell God what to do as it is to hear Him tell us what He wants to do. Those who listen to the Holy Spirit discern not only what to ask but also the fact that He hears them. Have you ever begun praying and, as you prayed, found your request changing because a different request seemed to be more pleasing to the Holy Spirit?

    c. The Spirit helps us desire deeply enough. When the Spirit of God guides us to desire a specific thing we can pray with faith, because God never burdens us to pray for anything He does not plan to answer. What is our promise in 1 John 5:15?

Listening

1. *Remove all distractions.* To hear God speak we need to quiet ourselves, because He speaks in "a still small voice." See 1 Kings 19:12, KJV.

Recently a young man told me he wanted to spend time alone with the LORD. "I'm not turning on any music or the radio," he said. To be silent before the Lord is not emptying our minds, but redirecting all thoughts to be centered upon God. See examples in the following passages of those who removed distractions so they could hear God.

 1 Kings 19:8-9

 Hab. 2:1

 Mark 1:35

How does it make you feel when someone you love says, "Listening to you is what I want to do most"?

"I wanted to spend time with the Lord, so I began taking my Bible to work, and I spent my lunch hour with Him," a friend said. "Afterward I had the distinct impression that He was pleased with my taking that time just to be with Him."

Her comments prompted me to add to my devotions a time simply to focus on God. Perhaps it's one form of what the psalmist David called "waiting on the Lord." I begin by praying, "Lord, I want my spirit to commune with Your Spirit." I'm often amazed at the sense of communion with the Holy Spirit that I experience during those times. I leave those times of silence strengthened in my spirit.

"Be still, and know . . ." (Ps. 46:10). There is a deep inner knowing in our spirits when we quiet ourselves in His presence. For most of us, the way to our inner being is through our hearts rather than our minds.

2. *Quiet your heart with worship.* Often the best way to do this is in praise and thanksgiving. In praise we become sensitive to the divine presence.

In God's presence the focus is not on one's own sins or problems. The focus is, "Worthy is the Lamb" (Rev. 5:12). If we want to be aware of His presence, we, too, must focus our thoughts on Him.

God is looking for worshipers. We tend to approach God as though He's looking for workers; but our heavenly Bridegroom is wooing a bride, not hiring a servant. He values our prayer and communion more than our labor and sacrifice. See Ps. 69:30-31.

3. *Be quick to hear, slow to speak.* In the Gospels, watching is given as a necessary prelude to prayer. (For instance, see Mark 14:38.) The Greek word for "watch" means "to be vigilant" and is taken from a word that means "to collect one's faculties." Early Quakers believed the purpose of this watching was to wait to feel God's Spirit draw them into prayer so they could pray acceptably.

The Quakers understood that we can do nothing without Christ, so they waited until they were moved by the Spirit before praying or speaking in their services. They spoke of "retiring inwardly to the Lord."[4] Of what value might it be to wait in silence, focusing on God before we begin praying?

It is foolish to rush into God's presence and ask the first thing that comes into our minds. When we first come to Him, we should be silent and look to Him to send His Spirit to teach us how to pray. As we surrender ourselves to the Spirit, we will pray correctly.

God wants us to listen for His voice, rather than get caught up in our own words. Don't we choose our words more carefully if we're listening closely to someone?

"Do not be quick with your mouth, do not be hasty in your heart to utter anything before God" (Eccles. 5:2). Why do you think we are to consider carefully what we say to God?

4. *Listen as you write.* Journaling can help both our listening and our petitioning in several ways:

    a. Writing our prayers can clarify our petitioning. "All this, said David, the LORD made me understand in writing by his hand upon me" (1 Chron. 28:19, KJV). Often as we write things down, new insights come. Writing slows us down so that we can think more carefully and choose our words more precisely, as we consider each detail that is important to us.

    b. We know precisely what we've asked of the Lord, and often this strengthens our ability to believe.

    c. Later as we reread our prayers, we'll be more aware of God's faithfulness to hear. Often when we read our exact request, we'll be amazed to see how precisely God answered. Frequently we forget past prayers; consequently, we don't recognize God's answers.

If you have tried writing your prayers, what benefits have you found?

5. Writing what God says to you provides a new freedom in hearing God's voice. Have you ever tried writing, not just your thoughts to the Lord, but also writing His response? Notice that in psalms such as 32:7-8; 91:13-14; and 95:8-9, the psalmist went from writing his thoughts to writing God's thoughts.

In your journaling, do more than write your thoughts to the Lord. Trust the Lord to give you the mind of Christ as you write what He is saying to you. The Holy Spirit is within you. Begin writing, trusting Him to give you His thoughts.

Scriptural Role Model

Often things that keep us from fellowship with Jesus seem legitimate. If I had been Zaccheus, would I have excused not seeing Jesus by saying, "But there were too many people, and I was too short"? Or would I have planned ahead as he did? "He ran before, and climbed up into a sycamore tree to see him" (Luke 19:4, KJV).

A strong desire to come into His presence is still rewarded with glimpses of Jesus.

Memorize
"Send forth your light and your truth, let them guide me; let them bring me to your holy mountain, to the place where you dwell" (Ps. 43:3).

Prayer
Open my eyes, Lord, to behold wondrous things in Your Law. I can do nothing on my own. Enable me to hear You, to see You, and to believe You are with me. Teach me to find that inner stillness that allows me to enjoy the fellowship of Your Spirit. In Jesus' name I pray. Amen.

APPENDIX

SUGGESTIONS FOR LEADERS

Prayerfully Prepare

If you have a desire to lead a Bible study, consider that desire to be a gift from God. "Delight yourself in the LORD and he will give you the desires of your heart" (Ps. 37:4). God never gives you a desire to do a task for Him without providing all you need to accomplish it. Your most important qualification for this role is a sense of dependence on the Lord for His perfect provisions.

Lorne Sanny said, "Prayer is the battle; witnessing is taking the spoils." It's just as true to say, "Prayer is the battle; leading a small group is taking the spoils." You will lead with more confidence if you have prayed until you are trusting God to do His work in the group. Through prayer you gain a sensitivity to the Holy Spirit, so you can allow Him to guide the discussion according to the needs of the group.

As you study, seek to find from the Word a truth that excites you. Your excitement for the Word will be contagious. The psalmist wrote, "Blessed is the man . . . who finds great delight in his commands" (Ps. 112:1). *The Living Bible* adds that such a person "shall have influence and honor" (v. 9, TLB).

If the truths you seek to share have reached only your intellect, they will likely reach only the intellect of those in your group also. But if the truths have reached your heart and changed your life, then there is a great chance they will reach the hearts of your group members and be life-changing for them as well.

Rely upon the Lord to be the Teacher, because spiritual truths must be taught by the Spirit. Isaiah 55:10 promises that the Word will be "seed for the sower and bread for the eater." Your role is simply to sow the seed. As you do, God promises to provide the miracle of turning it into bread for those who receive it. Before every group meeting, ask God to provide spiritual bread for each one coming.

In the Tabernacle, there was always to be "the bread of the Presence" on the table "at all times" (Exod. 25:30). As you trust Him, God will always provide the exact bread each member needs that day. When you are tempted to think your supply of seed is exhausted, claim 2 Cor. 9:10— "Now he who supplies seed to the sower and bread for food will also supply and increase your store of seed and will enlarge the harvest of your righteousness."

Lead with Confidence

Be willing to share how God has worked in your life. Paul asked that his listeners follow him as he followed Christ. "Whatever you have learned or received or heard from me, or seen in me—put it into practice" (Phil. 4:9). As you allow the group members to see how you follow Christ, you not only model for them how to follow Him but also provide the motivation. Many times Christians know what they must do to follow Christ, but simply need the leadership of one who is wholeheartedly committed to obedience. Be that person for those in your group.

Keeping the Bible study alive and friendly is imperative. Your own attitude is a key factor in the group's enthusiasm. Develop a genuine interest in each person's remarks, and expect to learn from each individual. Concentrate on developing acceptance and compassion in the group.

Don't be afraid of silence after asking a question. Give everyone time to think. Use "What do you think?" questions. It can help keep the discussion from seeming pressured or unnatural, since there is no such thing as a wrong answer to this type of question.

Remember that your goal is not simply to lead an interesting discussion but also to help group members understand and apply God's Word so it becomes life to them.

"They are not just idle words for you—they are your life" (Deut. 32:47).

Occasionally suggest, "Next week let's bring to our group the verses that have especially ministered to us." Usually a verse becomes special when it meets a personal need, so group members will often share these needs as well. Studying Scripture develops bonds of true friendship.

Remember Mal. 3:16 when enjoying the breaking of spiritual bread that occurs in group Bible studies: "Then those who feared the LORD talked with each other, and the LORD listened and heard. A scroll of remembrance was written in his presence concerning those who feared the LORD and honored his name." The Hebrew word for "listened" paints a picture of a mother bending over to listen to her children. Imagine God listening to you speak of Him and telling His recording angel to write your conversation in a journal in heaven!

"The lips of the righteous know what is fitting" (Prov. 10:32). Lead with confidence, because the Lord will help your words to be appropriate as you learn to depend on Him.

Practical Tips

"In his heart a man plans his course, but the LORD determines his steps" (Prov. 16:9). As you make plans to respond to the desires He has given, the Lord will direct your steps and provide the specific guidance needed.

Although these lessons assume that those who are studying them are Christians, welcome all who wish to join you. In the Early Church, the Lord added to their number. He is still Lord of the harvest and knows who to draw. He will give a desire to all those who should be a part of your group. Depend upon the Lord to direct those who would profit from the study to attend. Edith Schaeffer stated that the workers at L'Abri—a Swiss chalet opened by Francis and Edith for young people with philosophical questions—asked God to bring those who should come there to study and to keep away those who should not.[1] (It will be difficult for a majority to participate in the discussion, if the group is larger than 10 or 12.)

Unless you are meeting as a Sunday School class or other regularly scheduled meeting at church, the ideal setting would be the home of a hospitable member of the church. Trust the Lord for details regarding time and place for weekly group meetings. Perhaps you could meet once when everyone can come, and then determine the details.

If you, as the leader, come early, you do more than set a good example. You also communicate your enthusiasm and delight in the group.

Begin on time, even if not all members are present. Be sure chairs are set up for latecomers to easily join you. Don't ignore latecomers, but don't let them disrupt the session. Greet them warmly, and then return to the study.

If you decide to include refreshments, a sheet can be available at the first meeting inviting those to sign who would like to provide refreshments.

Begin with prayer. Prayer is more than a transition from small talk to Bible study. You are providing the group with a consciousness that they are in God's presence.

Give time for prayer requests either before the opening or the closing prayer. If someone has a special need, ask for volunteers who will spend 5 or 10 minutes during the next week in prayer for that person. Twelve 5-minute periods of prayer equal an hour of prayer! Send around a sheet of paper with the prayer request written on it, and ask group members to write down how many minutes they will pray, to help them feel that they have indeed committed themselves to prayer.

You may want to begin each session by reviewing memorized scripture. Encourage group members to write down the suggested verse, or a passage that challenges or encourages them, and reflect on it during the next week. They will find that verse beginning to affect their motives and actions. We forget quickly what we read once, but we remember what we ponder and act upon.

A few of the questions will be most easily understood if the *New International Version* is used.

Rather than moving mechanically through the written questions in each lesson, you may want to prepare some of your own questions. Write them out in advance and ask yourself if they are relevant and if the responses will teach what you think is important in the lesson. Avoid asking anything that is so personal the group members might find it threatening, unless you are willing to respond to the question first. As you share how God has convicted, encouraged, or instructed you through His Word, others will be drawn into sharing also.

End on time. If you say the study will be over at 9:00, end at 9:00. Then if any group members want to stay and visit, they can. This allows those with schedules to keep, or children to pick up to exit, without feeling they are missing part of the study.

Keeping in contact between weekly meetings is important. Make their burdens your own and let them know you are praying for them. When they are absent call to tell them you missed them, but don't pressure them to attend.

You are "God's workmanship, created in Christ Jesus to do good works, which God prepared in advance for us to do" (Eph. 2:10). All you need for this study has been pre-planned by Him.

Additional Chapter Comments

Chapter 1

Following Christ gives the only real joy that exists, and God has placed within each of us a hunger for this deep satisfaction. Jesus called this joy "life" and said His purpose for coming was to give abundant life to us (John 10:10).

Jesus defined life in John 17:3—"Now this is eternal life: that they may know you, the only true God." A lady told me, "I bought a Bible because I was hungry." Few people understand that their deepest longing is quenched with God's truth. Instead, they accept Satan's substitutes for joy, which are temporary and, in the end, empty. Solomon called all these efforts to obtain joy "meaningless." Following our own passions leads to death, but learning and doing the will of our Father leads to life.

"Feed on Him in your hearts by faith" is a phrase frequently used in Communion services. Encourage those in your group to develop the habit of keeping nourishing bits of truth readily available and to learn to feed on those. For instance, scriptures written on cards to read and obey throughout their day can become "real food" and "real drink" to their spirits.

Additional Notes:

Chapter 2

In discovering God's guidance, the law is "According to your faith will it be done to you" (Matt. 9:29). As in all else, the measure of what we receive from God is determined by our faith. Some Christians fail to see that God controls all their life, so without acknowledging that He does, they fail to trust Him. If we trust Him to be the Blessed Controller of our daily details, we'll find surprising evidences of Him throughout our day.

God leads us even when we are unaware of His guidance. He carefully weighs every burden He puts on us and will never put on us more than He can cause to work for our good and His glory.

When Habakkuk understood that God was sovereign, he listed the worst calamities he could imagine and said, "Yet I will rejoice in the LORD, I will be joyful in God my Savior" (Hab. 3:18). Habakkuk had reached the ultimate in spiritual growth; he could praise the Lord no matter what happened, because he recognized that he followed a sovereign God.

Encourage those in your group to trust God with the control of every detail of their daily lives and to praise God in all things. Emphasize that when God says He works all things together for good, He defines "good" as that which conforms us to the image of Christ. Ask them how that might differ from how *we* would define "good." See Rom. 8:28-29.

Additional Notes:

Chapter 3

The more we can say "I love You so much that all my other desires are second to my desire to give delight to You," the more we can see clearly how to follow Christ. Paul told the Philippians, "And this is my prayer: that your love may abound more and more in knowledge and depth of insight, so that you may be able to discern what is best" (Phil. 1:9-10). As our love for Christ and His will increases, our discernment increases.

There are levels of obedience, and at times we'll be tempted to remain at level one.

Level 1. I'd disobey if I could get by with it, but someone else or circumstances force me to do what is right.

Level 2. I choose Your will, but not willingly. I obey because I know it's right. My spirit is reluctant, so I pray to be made willing. "For it is God who works in you both to will and to do for His good pleasure" (Phil. 2:13, NKJV).

Level 3. I want to please You because Your pleasure is my highest joy. "I delight to do thy will, O my God" (Ps. 40:8, KJV). "All my fountains are in you" (Ps. 87:7). When Jesus said, "Father, glorify your name!" God replied, "I have glorified it, and will glorify it again" (John 12:28). God could not have said anything that would have satisfied Jesus more. When we have the mind of Christ, our deepest satisfaction will be in knowing that God is glorified.

Many times, humbling ourselves and deliberately choosing to have the mind of Christ will not be easy. You might want to discuss with your group the benefits of having a spirit of love and obedience even when it's difficult.

Additional Notes:

Chapter 4

Following God often means we are called to follow those He has placed around us. However, our limited perspective may cause us to wish for an alternate way to follow Him.

God does not always lead us down the easiest path. He knows our weaknesses and our temptations. When we think His guidance is calling us to submit to someone with whom we don't agree, it may be for our protection.

When Pharaoh let the Israelites go, God did not lead them on the road through the Philistine country, although that route was shorter. "For God said, 'If they face war, they might change their minds and return to Egypt'" (Exod. 13:17).

One of the key thoughts in this chapter is the definition of submission: trusting God to direct me through the authorities He has placed in my life. God will lead and protect us through those He has placed over us.

Submission is more about our response to God than our response to our authority. As in all of our Christian life, our faith in God is what is important. If we trust Him, He will lead us through those persons He places over us. You might want to ask the group members to share times when they submitted and discovered a surprising benefit.

Additional Notes:

Chapter 5

"Make sure you really want guidance, then hold steady and God will find a way of letting you know in the nick of time," promises Richard Taylor.[2]

To find God's guidance, we must be wholly committed to doing His will. If we have not actively put the responsibility into His hands, we'll be biased. Even if our bias is unconscious, it can easily mislead us. Martin Wells Knapp wrote, "Any mental reservation in the commitment will deaden the discerning of the divine voice."[3]

The best way to encourage personal sharing is for you to be willing to share how the Holy Spirit has spoken to your heart. Often we understand the right thing to do but need role models who can say, "Follow me as I follow Christ." It's easier to follow a pattern than an idea, so sharing how you apply scripture is an important part of your teaching.

Additional Notes:

Chapter 6

One of the most sacred statements in the New Testament is in Acts 15:28—"It seemed good to the Holy Spirit and to us . . ." This chapter is aimed at increasing our ability to discern what seems good to the Holy Spirit.

Our goal is to have the mind of Christ. At times we need to ask ourselves probing questions to see if our attitude is "the same as that of Christ Jesus" (Phil. 2:5). "The Holy Spirit will teach you," Jesus promised in Luke 12:12. It's not our learning or our wisdom that brings us God's truth, but a humble and teachable spirit.

At times we do recognize Him in our lives, but He yearns for us to be able to recognize His voice. He was pleased when Solomon made wisdom his priority request. See 1 Kings 3:5-14.

Just as Christ acted with His disciples while He was with them, so the Holy Spirit acts with us. Ask members of the group to consider if there are qualities they know to be in Jesus that can help them recognize the Holy Spirit's dealings.

Additional Notes:

Chapter 7

We all make mistakes, but God makes the best of our failures when we begin acting in obedience. The Old Testament shows God doing good to people who had gotten themselves into terrible trouble because of their own sin. See Ps. 107:10-13. The Lord is looking for people to bless, who despair of themselves and look wholly to Him for the help they need.

This chapter assumes that after we've failed, we've confessed our failure to God and asked for His forgiveness. Adam Clarke says the story of Balaam and an ass shows God's dealings with the unrepentant disobedient. See Num. 22:21-35.

First, God mildly shakes His rod at them but lets them go untouched.

Second, He comes nearer and touches them with an easy correction, as though He were forcing their foot against the wall.

Third, when that's ineffective, He brings them into situations in which they can turn neither to the right nor to the left but must fall before His judgments if they do not fully turn to Him.

You might want to ask each one of the group members to share the thought in this chapter that was the most comforting to him or her.

Additional Notes:

Chapter 8

The Spirit will help us develop Bible reading methods appropriate for us. While we may be tempted to say, "This is *the* method to use for Bible study," the Holy Spirit teaches each of us individually (1 John 2:27). Sometimes it helps us to share what works in our lives, or to listen to what others have discovered about hearing God.

In her autobiography *Hearing Heart,* Hannah Hurnard tells how she learned to hear God speak through His Word:

> He used my ordinary mental faculties and encouraged me to ask questions all the time. There was . . . no waiting for thoughts to come to me out of the blue. But He seemed to clarify my thoughts as I expressed my questions in words or in writing and enabled me to think the answers He wanted me to receive.
>
> Often of course it was just my own thoughts that came to me as I pondered on the subject I was reading each day, but I quickly became able to recognize His answers to my questions, for those thoughts came with a clarity and a kind of illumination which my own conclusions lacked. It was as though all of a sudden something clicked in my mind. "Ah, that's it; that is what He wants me to understand. That's what He wants me to do. So that is the meaning of this passage; why did I never see it before?" This of course gradually developed as I got up day after day for my quiet times."[4]

His speaking to us is very gentle: "My words descend like dew" (Deut. 32:2). Ask those in the group to share what has helped them recognize the Holy Spirit's voice speaking to them through the Word or through prayer.

Additional Notes:

Notes

Chapter 1

1. William Dyrness, *Themes in Old Testament Theology* (Downers Grove, Ill.: InterVarsity Press, 1979), 37.

2. Bernard Berkowitz and Mildred Newman, "How to Be Your Very Own Best Friend," *Bottom Line,* June 1, 1995, 1.

3. David H. Stern, *Jewish New Testament Commentary* (Clarksville, Md.: Jewish New Testament Publications, 1992), 174.

4. Ibid.

5. B. F. Westcott, *The Gospel According to St. John* (Grand Rapids: Wm. B. Eerdmans Publishing Co., 1973), 101.

6. Ibid.

Chapter 2

1. William Law, *The Heart of True Spirituality, John Wesley's Own Choice,* vol. 1 (Grand Rapids: Francis Asbury Press of Zondervan Publishing House, 1985), 84.

2. R. C. H. Lenski, *The Interpretation of St. Paul's Epistles* (Minneapolis: Augsburg Publishing House, 1937), 275.

3. Evelyn Christenson, *What Happens When God Answers Prayer* (Wheaton, Ill.: Victor Books, 1994), 188.

Chapter 3

1. Hannah Whitall Smith, *Everyday Religion* (Salem, Ohio: Allegheny Publications, 1988), 63.

2. George Watson, *Soul Food* (Cincinnati: Revivalist Office, 1896), 50.

3. Norman Grubb, *Rees Howells, Intercessor* (Fort Washington, Pa.: Christian Literature Crusade, 1952), 105.

Chapter 4

1. Dyrness, *Themes in Old Testament Theology,* 144.

Chapter 5

1. Hannah Hurnard, *Hearing Heart* (Wheaton, Ill.: Tyndale House Publishers, 1986), 45.

Chapter 6

1. Wesley Duewel, *Let God Guide You Daily* (Grand Rapids: Francis Asbury Press of Zondervan Publishing House, 1988), 124.

2. Thomas Upham, *Inward Divine Guidance* (Salem, Ohio: Schmul Publishing Company, 1989), 58.

3. Duewel, *Let God Guide You Daily,* 122.

Chapter 7

1. Richard S. Taylor, *Life in the Spirit* (Kansas City: Beacon Hill Press of Kansas City, 1966), 147.

2. Duewel, *Let God Guide You Daily*, 17.

3. Phoebe Palmer, *The Promise of the Father* (1859; reprint, Salem, Ohio: Schmul Publishers, 1981), 215.

4. Dick Eastman, *A Celebration of Praise* (Grand Rapids: Baker Book House, 1984), 131.

5. Catherine Marshall, *The Helper* (Grand Rapids: Chosen Books, 1978), 70-71.

Chapter 8

1. R. A. Torrey, *How to Pray* (Chicago: Bible Institute Colportage Association, 1900), 31.

2. Mark Virkler, *Dialogue with God* (South Plainfield, N.J.: Bridge Publishing, 1986), 147.

3. Duewel, *Let God Guide You Daily*, 82.

4. Dean Freiday, ed., *Barclay's Apology in Modern English* (Newberg, Oreg.: Barclay Press, 1967), 279.

Appendix

1. Edith Schaeffer, *L'Abri* (Wheaton, Ill.: Tyndale House Publishers, 1976), 124.

2. Taylor, *Life in the Spirit*, 137.

3. Martin Wells Knapp, *Impressions* (Cincinnati: Revivalist Publishing House, n.d.), 85.

4. Hurnard, *Hearing Heart*, 36.

OTHER BOOKS IN THE
SATISFIED HEART SERIES

SIMPLY TRUSTING
083-411-6049

Simply Trusting will guide you in deepening your faith and living with the confidence that God will answer your prayers.

BOLDLY ASKING
083-411-6057

Discover what it means to come boldly to God in joyous praise, to bring requests, and to expect the abundance of life devoted to unhindered prayer.

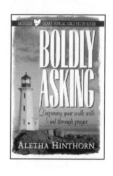

The Land of canaan christian living for the single [handwritten note]

QUIETLY RESTING
083-411-6073

Discover the peace that passes all understanding and the rest that God gives as a natural result of the truly Spirit-filled life.